What No One Ever Tells You About

RENOVATING YOUR HOME

Alan J. Heavens

Dearborn™
Trade Publishing
A **Kaplan Professional** Company

Vice President and Publisher: Cynthia A. Zigmund
Acquisitions Editor: Mary B. Good
Senior Project Editor: Trey Thoelcke
Interior Design: Lucy Jenkins
Cover Design: Scott Rattray, Rattray Design
Typesetting: the dotted i

Published by Dearborn Trade Publishing
A Kaplan Professional Company

Printed in the United States of America

05 06 07   10 9 8 7 6 5 4 3 2 1

Library of Congress Cataloging-in-Publication Data

Heavens, Alan J.
    What no one ever tells you about renovating your home / Alan J. Heavens.
      p.   cm.
    Includes index.
    ISBN 1-4195-0157-7
    1. Dwellings—Remodeling.   I. Title.
TH4816.H39 2005
643'.7—dc22

2004026172

Dearborn Trade books are available at special quantity discounts to use for sales promotions, employee premiums, or educational purposes. Please call our Special Sales Department to order or for more information at 800-621-9621 ext. 4444, e-mail trade@dearborn.com, or write to Dearborn Trade Publishing, 30 South Wacker Drive, Suite 2500, Chicago, IL 60606-7481.

To my wife, Ellen Gray—
she knows why.

CONTENTS

PREFACE

The debt I owe to my first contractor is greater than the $10,000 I paid him to wreck my first house 21 years ago.

The contractor, the brother of a friend, promised I could have anything I wanted. I got nothing I wanted. Just about every promise was broken. Still, we kept our end and paid him.

The ten-day job took six weeks. We assumed it was just about over when the toilet in the kitchen had been returned to the first-floor powder room. It still took a while for it to sink in that the contractor would never return. When I was absolutely convinced that the tile man who had been promised to me to finish the kitchen countertop also would never show, I licked my wounds, bought a book on drywall installation, and began tearing out the contractor's efforts to build a usable laundry room. I learned to tile, too.

After a few years and many more disappointments, I began sharing what I'd learned with the readers of the *Philadelphia Inquirer* and about 400 newspapers around the country.

I don't wish to mislead you. This is not a do-it-yourself book in the sense that you'll be able to drywall a kitchen when you finish it. What I'm hoping you'll come away with is a sense of empowerment that will put you, the consumer, in complete control of the renovation process from the moment an idea pops into your head to the day that your idea, or an acceptable version of it, can be seen, touched, and enjoyed.

Instead of teaching you how to drywall, I want to provide the skills you need to hire the right drywall contractor, to determine whether you want new drywall or restored plaster, and to understand the basics of the job and get exactly what you're paying for—or know the reason why you don't. Most how-to books oversimplify drywall installation anyway. Most professionals typically do it better, faster, and less expensively than a do-it-yourselfer. I know. I've done my own for 22 years. Each time I'm finished, I ask myself why I didn't pay someone to do it.

That doesn't mean I'm an enemy of doing it yourself, just that you should rely on common sense when deciding what jobs you want to take on. If you think you will learn something or want to have something to be proud of, go right ahead. If you think you'll save money, think twice, especially if you don't know what you are doing. You are bound to spend more.

According to Bob Pares of the Roper Organization, *do-it-yourself* has come to mean more than just picking up a hammer. *Do-it-yourself* has become "a feeling of self-reliance." Consumers want to inject themselves into the process so they can exercise greater control and ensure a better outcome, no matter what the situation is. For most consumers, *doing it yourself* is more "knowing it yourself" or "managing it yourself." Knowledge is the key to self-reliance.

I also hope that the contractors who read this book get a sense of how we consumers think and feel and that they adjust their attitudes and business practices accordingly. I'm not trying to hypnotize contractors into believing that the customer is always right. Nor am I saying that contractors are always wrong. I'm simply saying that there is a middle road to success, and I hope I'm able to show you that way.

The willingness to listen and to compromise is what raises statesmen above the level of politicians. That same willingness to meet your contractor halfway, and for the contractor to meet you there as well, will guarantee success for your renovation project.

Your home is the biggest investment you'll ever make. Any change you make to your home should increase your investment, not subtract from it. Too often, however, we do the wrong thing. We add on when we should move. We embark on projects that make our house too expensive for the neighborhood. We spend more money on a project than we can possibly get back. We get into more debt than we can handle. We leave needed repairs unattended and devote our energies instead to insignificant projects.

You can't be right all of the time. You have to expect to make mistakes. If you didn't make them, you wouldn't be human. If you didn't err, you wouldn't learn.

If I spent this book sharing all the renovation mistakes I've made in the last 25 years, there would be room for nothing else. I have many regrets, but I've also never gotten myself into a situation that couldn't be solved, either with time or by throwing money at it. My goal is to help you avoid doing either.

Don't be scared. Just try to be smarter.

When I was seven, I saw Bela Lugosi in the 1931 classic film, *Dracula,* on television. I slept with a nightlight for many weeks. I've watched the movie hundreds of times since, and I can't understand what frightened me so much. In fact, I find myself laughing in a lot of places, because I'm older and smarter.

Homeownership, too, requires a sense of humor, as well as an occasional visit to the therapist, physical or otherwise. No matter how careful you are, something is bound to break or need replacing or maintenance. The longer you wait to act, the worse things will get. So swallow hard, shrug your shoulders, and smile. Then get it fixed, whether you do it yourself or hire someone to do it for you.

The bottom line: You can do this. By the time you reach the last page of this book, you'll be able to do anything or at least find someone who is able to do it for you.

Experience is the best teacher, so dare to try new things. Expect to make mistakes, because it's the best way to learn. And, if you'd like to share your ideas and experiences with me, feel free to e-mail me at aheavens@phillynews.com, or check out my articles and columns at http://www.philly.com/mld/philly/living/columnists/al_heavens/.

ACKNOWLEDGMENTS

I would like to thank a series of supportive and enthusiastic real estate editors, including Joanne McLaughlin, Barbara Matthews-Bowen, Lisa Tracy, Denise Cowie, and David I. Turner as well as James F. Moffatt, who showed me how to "put myself in the reader's place." I also wish to thank the thousands of readers in the United States and Canada who have taken time to praise me, question me, and, quite often, put me in *my* place.

Finally, I am deeply indebted to Nicholas Gray Heavens, my older son, for his invaluable assistance with the technology involved in getting the first and final drafts of this book to the publisher, and to Patrick Gray Heavens, my younger son, for his patience during the writing of this book.

RIGHT FROM THE START

. . .

Fools rush in where angels fear to tread.

That aptly describes how I approached home renovation in the early years. If there was a mistake to be made, I made it. Of course, I learned from my mistakes, but the pain involved made me wonder if it was worth it.

In retrospect, it was worth it.

My problem was that I didn't have it right from the start. My wife and I picked the wrong house in the wrong neighborhood because we hadn't done our homework. We didn't have the financial resources to renovate a fixer-upper. There was so much wrong, in fact, that we were only able to repair, not improve.

We didn't we have the expertise to do the work ourselves. We seemed to hire the wrong people to work for us. When we sold that house in a down real estate market, we couldn't recover what we had spent to fix it. We should have held on to the house as rental property until values increased, but we couldn't afford two mortgages for a prolonged period. So we turned around and bought another fixer-upper, which immediately began swallowing great chunks of our paychecks.

Part 1 reflects our early experiences and those of others. I hope it helps you approach homeownership and home renovation with a clearer head than I started with.

There are highs and lows in homeownership. Focus on the highs, but be aware of the potential problems.

Remember, the only way to avoid a pothole is to keep your eyes on the road.

1. IS THIS TRIP REALLY NECESSARY?

You need an ironclad reason to renovate.

■ ■ ■

You know you've lived in one place too long when you start renovating space that really doesn't need work. Maybe you've spent so much time fixing what's broken, you need to create or go mad. Maybe you've simply developed so much momentum that you can't stop yourself from working.

Or maybe it's time to talk to someone who can help you get control of yourself. It could be a therapist. In my case, it was a long-suffering spouse with a clear head.

I was renovating the basement, creating a family room and an accessible bathroom. The problem: We already had decided to move. My younger son has Down syndrome, and we were well aware that we'd be running out of private school options at the end of the school year. We needed to move to another town with a more useful school system, so we needed to finish all the projects I had started over the past 14 years as well as make many necessary repairs—or at least wash the windows.

And yet, there I was: in the basement, building walls.

"Don't you think it would be a better use of your time to finish painting the half-painted third-floor and second-floor hallways?" my wife asked me. "You need to do some painting, landscaping, and roof repair, finish the crown molding in the kitchen, fix the bottom stair of the deck, replace the latticework between our yard and the neighbor's, trim the trees, tear out the dead shrubs, get the porch downspout draining again, and coat the pole gutters on the third floor so they won't leak into the second floor bedroom."

I guess I was hoping for an academic miracle that would allow us to remain in our high-maintenance house forever. By my reckoning, we had spent $80,000 in 14 years. Hearing my wife list the jobs that still needed to be done convinced me that we weren't any nearer to being finished than when we had started. And then, for some reason, I had gotten it into my head that we needed to finish a basement that was damper than a sponge in a bucket of water.

It was time to move, and we did, even though I continued to work on the basement in some poorly thought-out effort to finish it before the house went on the market. I never did finish, and I'm sure the new owners, overwhelmed by the same maintenance issues that had overwhelmed me, continue to wonder what possessed me to start an obviously unnecessary project of that scope.

TV carpenter Norm Abram tells us to measure twice so that we only have to cut once. With renovation projects, experience teaches that by thinking twice, you may not have to cut at all. Yet, as I've shown you, it is difficult to be talked out of something once you have made up your mind.

When you buy a house, old or new, you must establish priorities based on what projects will make it livable and comfortable. After living in the house for a few months, you can use firsthand experience to rework the list. Meanwhile, you can make cosmetic changes that make the house feel more like home, such as repainting walls and hanging pictures. You can do these things yourself, because they don't cost much money. You probably have little to spare after buying the house, and you need to keep as much as you can in reserve for emergencies, such as clogged drains, heating and cooling system repairs, or storm damage.

Once you've made it this far and have established priorities, you can pick a major project and begin outlining what you want to do and what probably is unnecessary. Or, think twice, then make the necessary cuts, if you have to cut at all.

Let's look at your kitchen. Say that the kitchen is outdated and not very workable. Of course, most people want a $60,000 kitchen with two dishwashers and a stove—the kind of kitchen you'd only find in restaurants. You are no exception. How will spending $60,000 on just one room affect how much you can do for the rest of the house?

Look at your neighbors' kitchens. What will be the long-term benefits of having the best kitchen on the street? Will it price your house beyond what potential buyers are willing to pay? How will you use your kitchen? Will you use it to produce meals worthy of Wolfgang Puck, or will it be Pop-Tart City in the morning and Chinese takeout in the evening?

Try to find less expensive ways of making the space attractive and workable without a great expenditure of time and money. If you have little workspace but enough room, a worktable similar those in restaurant kitchens might provide plenty of food-preparation surface. The worktable can double as a dining area simply by purchasing four inexpensive stools.

How well do your appliances work? If you want a dishwasher and have no room for a permanent fixture, a portable can be stored easily when not in use. If any appliances need replacing, consider doing it now. Energy-efficient appliances, though expensive initially, will save you money in the long run. If you prefer a gas range to an electric one, a plumber and electrician can help determine how to cost-effectively disconnect one and install the other.

The electrician should look at the lighting while at your house. Determine where and how much it would cost to add lighting and eliminate shadows. The plumber can look at the water supply lines and drainage to see if they need replacing or upgrading.

A coat of paint can bring all the elements of the room together. That's also true of the flooring. It's relatively inexpensive to upgrade flooring by covering unsalvageable, faded linoleum with new, versatile vinyl.

You can do the project over time. That way, you don't have to spend months cooking in a toaster oven or lugging water for coffee from the bathroom sink. A phased project helps control costs better. It may mean, however, that you will be susceptible to price increases and materials shortages.

The biggest expenditure in most kitchens is cabinetry—about 45 percent of the total cost. Determine whether you can live with the cabinets you have or can add to their number without compromising the look you want. Consider painting the cabinets and buying new hardware. Not every old cabinet door can hold a coat of paint. You first have to determine what the cabinet is made of and see whether the old finish can be stripped or sanded or just roughed up and primed to hold the paint.

You also can change the color of the kitchen or bathroom tiles with acrylic paint, especially if those tiles are in good condition. The cost of replacing them can be better spent on a larger tub or new shower, but consider all options and potential drawbacks before you act.

Such cosmetic changes can be a do-it-yourself job. Still, the job needs to be done correctly to be successful. For the first two years, for example, the painted cabinets may look good, but sometimes they can start to chip and look worse than they did before you painted them. Then you are back in the market for kitchen cabinets. After saving money for a couple of years, however, you might be able to afford better cabinets and, indeed, a better kitchen than if you had rushed into major renovations right away.

I know, I know. Good things come to those who wait.

2. TO MOVE OR NOT TO MOVE

If renovating won't solve a problem, it is probably time to go.

■ ■ ■

Rule number one: Never renovate to sell.

Rule number two: If you have recently renovated and then decide to sell, you haven't really violated rule number one. In fact, you get the Savvy Homeowner Prize.

This week's winners: Alice and Terence Sexton.

Alice and Terence were perfectly happy in their house, which Terence had inherited from his parents and had invested a considerable amount of time and money in renovating. The couple fully expected that they and their two children—Danny, 5, and Tierney, 2—would live there for many years.

"We really did a lot of work on it," said Alice. "We tore out the linoleum and carpet in the kitchen and put in hardwood floors. While we were at it, we had the hardwood floors in the rest of the house refinished, painted the yellow pine cabinets, and painted the paneling around the fireplace in the kitchen." (Yes, Virginia, the kitchen had a fireplace.)

If that wasn't enough, they repaired a rotting subfloor in the main bath. Well, it really wasn't enough, and they ended up gutting the whole thing and starting over, removing the tiled bath and installing a one-piece fiberglass shower/tub, and replacing a 60-inch vanity, medicine cabinet, mirrors, and the toilet. Oh, and they added wainscoting. A "little" bathroom was restored to what Alice calls a "normal" look, which means that they removed the dropped ceiling that had been installed to cover the mistakes of a previous home improvement contractor.

All this and more in a year and a half.

Then two issues arose, as issues always seem to. First, the open space behind their house was targeted for high-density housing, meaning that on a clear day you'd probably be able to see into your neighbor's bathroom. Second, Danny was heading to kindergarten, and Alice and Terry were not impressed with the school district. They also didn't like the fact that kindergarten was only a half day. Because both were lawyers with unpredictable schedules, they'd still be spending money sending the boy to childcare for part of the day.

They put their house on the market, and it sold quickly. They bought a ranch-style home on an acre nearer to Alice's job and in an excellent school district. The new house needs a lot of work, Alice says, but they have plenty of time to decide what they want and when and how they want to do it.

You may be asking yourself if they regret having to move, especially after spending all that money on improvements they were just beginning to enjoy and when they face the prospect of doing the same things in another house. No, they don't regret it.

"When we replaced the kitchen counters with laminate, we also installed an extra deep sink," Alice said. "We still miss that sink, although eventually we'll install one in this kitchen."

Let's say that you've outgrown your living quarters and like where you live, but you cannot afford the larger houses in your neighborhood or community or in another town. You do have options. You can add on, or you can turn existing space you've never thought of using into bedrooms or bathrooms. Before you expand, however, you have to consider the physical, legal, and financial aspects.

Say you want a two-story addition to accommodate a second-floor master suite and a family room on the first floor. Do you have enough property to do it and still meet local planning and zoning regulations? What about the neighbors? They will want a say in something that might block the sun from their gardens or affect property values, taxes, and resale value. If you've never thought as far as resale, consider it before you act.

Don't overenlarge. In a neighborhood full of three-bedroom houses that attract small families, how quickly will your five-bedroom house sell?

Two-story additions should blend with the original structures. Matching stone is always the toughest. Brick is easier, because used brick is often available in older areas. It is much more expensive than new brick, however, because old mortar has to be cleaned from the surfaces of the older brick.

If an addition does not work for you, why not look into the attic and the basement? The annual "Cost versus Value" report published by *Remodeler* magazine shows that creating an air-conditioned attic bedroom—a 15-by-15-foot room with a 5-by-7-foot shower bath—averages $22,840 nationally, and that 84 percent of that money will be recouped at resale time. The attics of some houses are often crawl spaces, so the roofs may need to be bumped out to create headroom. You have to consider how doing so will change the roofline and thus the look of the house.

Although resale might not be an issue here—extra space can mean a home office, a guest room, or a playroom for families not needing an extra bedroom—you will need to contact the local building official to see what kind of permits are needed. Changing the exterior of the house might require planning and zoning approvals. Don't forget to bring your neighbors into the process at the start.

What about basements? When people buy older houses, one of the first places they think of expanding into is the basement. One of the first questions they ask is whether the basement is wet or dry. Although a finished basement is just one item on a buyer's wish list, it sometimes can make or break a resale. Uses for finished basements include exercise rooms, home offices, and storage.

New home buyers have it a little easier, because houses are coming with what are called "bonus rooms." Actually, they are not rooms—just spaces that will become something when the homeowner needs them. Bonus space is probably one of the more popular options in new construction, because it gives the buyer the option of having room to grow without having to decide at sale time what to build or pay up front for finished space.

Although tastes vary from region to region, there are some shared preferences. One is house size. The National Association of Home Builders has found that buyers in all regions are looking for houses with more than 2,200 square feet of living space. They also prefer to pay no more than $200,000 for whatever they buy. That's where the similarities end, however. What people in different regions want, and the changes they will make to get what they want, can differ greatly.

For example, homeowners in the Northeast tend to favor formal spaces more than their counterparts in California. There is a marked preference for a formal living room, even though it is hardly ever used and has evolved merely into a place that collects dust. That goes as well for the formal dining room, which is only used on holidays. It would never occur to someone in Nutley, New Jersey, in need of extra room to enlarge a kitchen to take it out of the dining room. Neither would a homeowner in Stamford, Connecticut, who wanted to create a family room ever consider combining the living room and dining room.

Their concern is resale. They believe they can't do without a living room when they when they eventually put the house on the market. This idea is, of course, encouraged by real estate agents lacking in creative marketing skills and by builders who don't want to rock the boat and their tight profit margins. Instead, to add a few hundred feet to the house, the typical Northeast homeowner will add a two-story addition that is much more expensive and much more jarring to the eye than if they had taken a chance with the living room or dining room.

What's missing is creativity and a sense of adventure. I'm not guaranteeing that people who take a chance will be rewarded, but you shouldn't do everything with an eye toward unloading the house at a moment's notice. For every house, there are three buyers. That is true for the traditional house as well as for the not-so-traditional.

I'd rather live in a house with little style, something that people will talk about instead of yawn about. What about you?

3. MAKE HASTE SLOWLY

Live in the house before deciding what needs to be done.

■ ■ ■

Sometimes, understandably enthusiastic first-time homebuyers jump into extensive and costly renovation projects just a few days after they walk in the front door for the first time. They later end up with much more than the new bathroom they wanted.

Why? Inexperience, compounded by enthusiasm. Our society seems to thrive on instant gratification. We want it now, even if it puts us in a financial hole.

First-time buyers are typically tight upon closing and have little money left to play with for at least a year. More than half of first-time buyers choose older, less-expensive houses. Even buyers of new homes want to make changes when they walk in the front door, however. If they are not starry-eyed but thinking straight, these new-comers would be wiser to make cosmetic changes than spend $25,000 to turn a functioning, not-horrible bathroom into one that Cleopatra would have considered extravagant.

Listen carefully. In the first year, first-time buyers should focus on small projects, perhaps changing the color of the walls or refinishing hardwood floors. Painting is the number-one improvement by first-timers. Repainting is usually motivated more by taste than by necessity. A lot of buyers, first-time or otherwise, may buy a house despite the color of the walls, then head to the paint store as soon as the papers are signed. Surprisingly, so do new-home buyers. Builders use relatively inexpensive, generic brands of paint to cover the walls, because they assume, correctly, that buyers will repaint early on.

Another inexpensive way for first-timers to personalize their new digs is with window treatments. Venetian blinds can be replaced with curtains, shades, roman blinds, or minis.

Remodeling surveys by the Joint Center for Housing Studies at Harvard University and by the National Association of Home Builders show that first-timers under the age of 35 spend $2,070 a year on renovation projects. The amount climbs to $4,820 for people making $120,000 or more.

American Express Company compiles a retail index annually on home improvement trends. The reason cited most frequently for making exterior and interior alterations is "personal taste." If money were no object, project choices would include adding a room, building a porch or deck, completely rebuilding the house, and installing a swimming pool.

A big caveat: If you don't plan to live in the house for long, don't overimprove. Be careful not to spend more than you can recoup when you sell, especially if you are planning to occupy the house for only a short time. Make choices that will yield results that meet your own needs and are consistent with upgrades in other houses in your neighborhood.

During the first year, then, buyers should be make simple, inexpensive changes to their houses. If the only issue was money, we could drop this discussion, but another important reason for such prudence should be obvious: only after living in a house for a reasonable length of time can you make informed decisions about improvements. No matter how well the house fared in the inspection, and no matter how conscientious the previous owner was about maintenance, something always goes wrong in that first year.

During the inspection of my first house, I was lectured about how to maintain my water heater, to which the inspector gave a clean bill of health. "If you drain the heater every six months and remove the sediment that collects at the bottom, the water heater should last forever," he said. We replaced the heater a week after we moved in. The advice was sound, as most homeowners will attest, but water heaters have a life expectancy of eight to ten years, depending on how well you care for them and just plain luck.

If your home inspector provided you with a list of recommendations, tackle those jobs first, in order of importance.

What role does a contractor play in a homebuyer's life that first year? If you can get one to return your phone calls, the contractor should be both teacher and hand-holder, very much like your real estate agent. For example, say you are a first-time buyer and want to add some built-in bookcases. If the contractor notices that the roof needs repair or replacement, they should talk the buyer out of the bookcases for now to focus on the roof.

A contractor has to work with first-time buyers so they can learn to establish priorities. For contractors, this is a chance to build a relationship of trust. In the long run, that means repeat business and word of mouth referrals to friends and neighbors.

What jobs do first-time buyers do themselves the first year? Do-it-yourself projects include hanging pictures, hooking up washers and dryers or the cable-TV box, fixing squeaky or sticking doors and drawers, and tending to small plumbing problems that might not require a plumber. These are perfect tasks to be handled by first-timers with little or no experience, because they save money and build confidence.

Problems arise when you embark on a do-it-yourself project that is well above your abilities. Other common mistakes include hiring the wrong contractor, selecting inferior products to save money, improper planning, not taking all choices into consideration, starting the project at the wrong time, and not managing your budget. Another mistake is "the domino effect." For example, you might install a new kitchen, then decide the living room looks shabby, and so on, until you break your budget.

I know, I know. You want to get the house of your dreams yesterday. However, to dream, you need to sleep—or at least close your eyes and rest for a while. Unless your hot water heater goes the first week you're in the house, you can afford to take it easy, look around, and consider your options.

The Roman Emperor Augustus had a saying, "Make haste slowly." That's probably the reason Rome wasn't built in a day.

4. MAYBE IF YOU CLEANED UP A LITTLE

All you need to do is throw out and then reorganize.

■ ■ ■

Running out of room? Perhaps you just have too much "stuff." If you are saving the clothes you wore in high school—maybe they'll fit if they ever come back in style—getting rid of them may open up enough space that you don't have to build another closet. Maybe the dead electronic equipment occupying shelves in the basement can be recycled. And how many easy chairs does one living room really need?

Census statistics show that the typical American family is getting smaller, yet the space we need to live continues to grow. In the 1980s, children's rooms in new houses were small, because builders were giving more space to the master suites and his-and-her closets. That didn't last. These days, children's rooms are two or three times the size they were 20 years ago.

Why? Stuff. Houses have gotten larger to accommodate the need for space, but we don't just seem to need space. We need change just as much. Space and change don't have to mean an expensive addition or moving. Getting rid of things you don't need, or simply rearranging your prized possessions, can give you the same feeling for much less.

There are businesses that do "facelifts" and makeovers of rooms for much less than full-scale renovations, yet accomplish pretty much the same thing. This is not interior design, which involves coming up with rooms from scratch. This is taking the contents of a room or house and creating a whole new look simply by rearranging things. The theory is that most people don't know what to do with what they own, so they stuff rooms and closets with dust-collecting—pardon the expression—junk.

I suppose that creatively rearranging things in your rooms can help, especially if you take pieces and arrange them to achieve some sort of balance, putting the things you want to highlight where everyone can see them and where they look best while finding appropriate, less obtrusive spaces for the rest of your possessions. Rearranging can be as easy as removing a second chair from the living room, which also can make a small room look more spacious—a technique real estate agents use when they show houses to buyers.

The art of rearranging is often used to blend possessions when two separate households are combined—for example, when two older persons marry and assemble the contents of two houses into one. Often, they don't choose the bigger house to combine into, so they need a plan.

I was a bachelor well into my late 20s and was convinced that I would remain so. After living for several years with furniture that relatives and friends had cast off, I decided to spend some money on higher-quality stuff that fit my stodgy lifestyle. The term *higher-quality* is a misnomer. The furniture was expensive, but it was not particularly well made and was very dark, heavy, and horribly middle class. Just as I finished buying the last piece, I met my future wife. A few months later, I moved to a smaller apartment, and a lot of the furniture I had acquired was given to friends and relatives. That process quickened after we were married, because my taste wasn't my wife's, and, frankly, hers was better.

Taste wasn't the only determinant and certainly wasn't the most important one. That was space. I'd bought all that furniture for a two-bedroom apartment, then moved to a one-bedroom place. Just after we were married, we both got new jobs in a new city, so we took the contents of both of our apartments on the road, finally jamming them into a 1,100-square-foot house. We spent the next six years giving away a lot of furniture and adding smaller pieces, including baby furniture.

Then we bought a 3,500-square-foot house and started acquiring furniture to fill six bedrooms. After 14 years of adding to our possessions, we bought a 2,000-square-foot house and found ourselves getting rid of everything that hadn't proved worth keeping. In one weekend, my wife filled 16 trash bags full of clothes. We gave away beds, dressers, sideboards, desks, and chairs. When we were done, we looked around the house we were about ready to vacate. We realized that it looked so much better without all that stuff—much more livable. Because we threw away so much, the new house is minimalist and comfortable, and everything has a place.

Still, we had a hard time deciding what to get rid of, and sometimes I think maybe we went a little overboard. However, the statement made by stuff piled ceiling-high on the floors of musty basements is not a pleasant one, says Leslie Robison of Green Lane, Pennsylvania, who owns a firm called Simple Systems Organizing and counsels homeowners on how to reduce clutter.

"People spend years collecting papers and craft items they think will be valuable one day, but there ends up being so much of it, that they can't recall why they saved it in the first place," she says. So Robison, for an hourly fee, helps them declutter. "Clutter is the result of people losing control of things. So I come in and locate the stuff in the backs of closets and cabinets and try to move it closer to places where it will be used."

Clutter is primarily created by busy lives. Americans are working long hours, and when they come home, they don't really want to clean the closets and cabinets. They just dump stuff they carry in the house on any available flat surface. That's why no one is eating at a lot of dining room tables.

Computers have doubled the problem with paper because only one side is being used, and too many people are not reading e-mail on the screen but print it and then read it.

By the time most people have reached their 40s and 50s, they have been collecting stuff without pause for more than 20 years. Garages hold a collection of bikes and lawn equipment instead of cars. That's when Leslie Robison comes in. "I help coordinate," she says. "They need less, but they have a hard time deciding what should go and what should stay."

While it seems perfectly logical that if you have too much stuff, you should get rid of it, a great deal of emotion is attached to some of these possessions. "If I show them something and they touch it, they tend to keep it," Robison says, "but if I show it to them and they don't touch, but tell me a story about it, they let it go."

Robison won't work with people who can't make changes, because she can't accomplish the job. She has to work *with* the client. In Robison's line, the client makes the decisions, not the consultant.

Robison works with people of all ages, especially those who have lost spouses. "We separate possessions into 'active' and 'inactive' areas," she says. But often what Robison and others might consider inactive do not seem inactive to the client. "I once worked with a woman whose son had died," she says. "I suggested that we put the son's grade school papers into the inactive pile. But the woman put them into the active pile because, for her, they were."

The goal is to get possessions under a reasonable limit, then arrange them so they are accessible. The rest can go out on the curb marked "free" or be featured in a yard sale. Your unwanted clutter will get a new lease on life, cluttering someone else's house.

5. NONE BUT THE BRAVE

It takes a certain kind of person to buy a fixer-upper.

■ ■ ■

I was dragged into homeownership kicking and screaming. My accountant stood over me, waving my 1981 federal return, telling me that if didn't get some sort of big deduction, Uncle Sam could afford to take early retirement based on what I was paying the government in income taxes.

Or it was something like that. I was perfectly happy in an apartment, leaving the worries about leaky roofs and shoveling snow to someone else in return for $600 a month. In addition, this was 1981, and fixed interest rates on mortgages were about 18 percent. Sure, my wife and I had the income to buy a house, but unless it was really cheap, we couldn't afford the payments unless we took on second jobs.

"So buy a house and fix it up," my accountant said. "You live in a city with lots of available housing stock, and the prices are real reasonable. You are a smart guy, and, what's better, your wife is a heck of a lot smarter than you are. So get moving so you can have that interest rate deduction on next year's return."

We looked, and looked, and looked, and looked, and . . . you get the picture. It wasn't easy finding something we liked that we could afford, as is true with many first-time buyers. Then my wife, poring over the real estate ads in the Sunday paper, found a house that had our name, or at least our numbers, attached to it. "For $10,000 down, you can assume a 13½ percent Veterans Administration mortgage on this attractive, three-bedroom house."

The house was in a neighborhood that was touted as up and coming, meaning that we might expect a return on our investment. We jumped on it. Nice house from the outside, OK inside, and only a block from the worst public housing project in the city. With our accountant waving that tax return in our face, with our savings account holding enough for the down payment and the closing costs, and with long-term and short-term mortgage interest rates showing no sign of falling below 18 percent any time soon, we jumped in feet first—and ended up treading water for the next six years.

A week after we moved in, the hot water heater, pronounced in fine shape by the home inspector a month before, had to be replaced. He had also said the roof was great. I don't even want to go there. I will say that the hot water heater was the least of our worries over the next six years.

Before I proceed, let me say that no matter how smart you think you are, you aren't as smart as you think. We didn't know this house was a fixer-upper when we bought it. We had been led to believe by the home inspector that we hired—when hiring one was not as common as today—that we were buying a real charmer, a house into which the previous owner had put tender loving care from which we would benefit. We should have waited and found other ways to reduce our tax burden. We were not handy, and we had just emptied our savings account. We also discovered, a couple of weeks after settlement day, that our first child was on the way.

The bottom line: We made a mistake that haunted us for years. When we moved six years later, I calculated that I had spent $30,000 on fixing up a house that had cost us $64,000. When we sold it six months after buying our next house, it brought $84,000, meaning that I had, on paper, lost $10,000. Because we had no real equity, we bought another fixer-upper several times larger than the first, which cost us almost three times more to turn around over the next 14 years.

Fortunately, bad luck doesn't necessarily have to last a lifetime. When we decided to move again—for reasons related to educating our two sons—we happened to hit a booming real estate market in a neighborhood that had truly changed. When we sold the house, we were able buy one that required no work unless I chose to make improvements.

I've presented what I consider the worst-case scenario, because I want you to think long and hard before you buy a house. In a sellers' market, such as the one we've been experiencing for more than five years, too many buyers, in their desperation to beat the competition for housing, race through an open house and then hand a signed check to the owner's agent. The sale is contingent on nothing, not a home inspection or even a second visit. Then, after closing, the buyers show up with new curtains and discover that the house doesn't have windows. I know this sounds extreme, but I'm trying to make a point.

No matter how good something seems to be, it never is. If you want to buy a fixer-upper, that should be a conscious decision. You need to take a number of factors into consideration before you make what can often be a painful leap. You should first decide whether the neighborhood and the house are both worth any money you spend, whether it is a few thousand dollars or a few hundred thousand dollars. You also need to consider what the house will need and whether you can hire people to take care of it or if you can do it yourself.

Most of all, you need to think long and hard about how disruptive such a project can be on your life, your family, and your job. Surviving for several years in dust and dirt with bathrooms and kitchens in unrecognizable pieces is no way to live, let me tell you. It takes a toll on you and your family. You find that, instead of watching your son play soccer, you are rushing to repair a roof before the next rainstorm. You have to make hard decisions about where you will spend your limited funds.

That's the bad news. Now, here's an illustration of the right way to go about home improvement.

Unlike me, Jim McGowan knew what he was getting into when he bought his 1,200-square-foot fixer-upper six years ago. He sought an investment property, picked a neighborhood that was up and coming, and looked long and hard for a house that he could turn around and not lose money as well as enjoy living in.

The house that he bought in a bank foreclosure sale was "something affordable that I could fix up," McGowan said. A painter for 20 years, he knew a lot about plumbing and was eager to tackle any job except electricity. It was a lot of work, but the price was right.

McGowan picked the right property. He had the expertise and was willing to spend the time. He had something else, something I consider more important than anything else: McGowan could see past the wreck that he had just bought to the house it could become. He had to strain his eyes to see past the kitchen with two metal cabinets and the cast-iron, porcelain-coated sink; the jalousie windows and the dirty linoleum; the sagging, wavy ceilings and the pink and gray plastic tiles in the only bathroom—but he was able to see the potential.

Six years later, with a house that he spent three years ripping apart and rebuilding from the joists and studs out, he had no regrets. He does have plenty of stories, but surprisingly, just one would fit the "horror" category.

"I took down an archway in the kitchen to rebuild it and tried to remove the wood trim carefully to save it," McGowan said. "The trim was old and cracked, and I couldn't save it. So I used seven gallons of joint compound instead to try to make the archway look good. A couple of days later, there was a heavy rain, and water came through the box where the gutter and the downspout meet and down the back bedroom wall into the kitchen wall and then into the archway, which collapsed. I had to do it over again."

Unlike most fixer-upper buyers, Jim didn't have to live in the house during the worst of the work. For the first year, every evening after work, he'd shut off his tools, turn off the lights, lock the doors, and go back to his apartment, shaking the grime and plaster dust from his feet rather than having to sleep covered with it.

Unfortunately, most fixer-upper buyers don't have that luxury. Allan M. Hasbrouck, who bought a big fixer-upper in the late 1970s, didn't. During the next ten years, he and his wife "substantially rebuilt the plumbing and electrical systems, put a new roof on the house, rebuilt the wraparound front porch, and did a complete cosmetic remake of the interior. The original workmanship was excellent, and so we really did not need, or want, to do any renovations. Restoration was what we were after."

The front-porch reconstruction was his greatest trauma. The porch was in the post-Victorian tradition, a large, L-shaped delight that wrapped around the front and side of the house. It was furnished with old wicker furniture inherited from his grandparents, and his family used it frequently on warm evenings to enjoy each other's company. However, it was getting rot. The tongue-in-groove decking was warped and split. The wooden Doric columns—ten of them grouped into pairs—were splitting and bowing. The box beams overhead were deteriorating. The steps were shaky. The porch needed help.

In all, 600 square feet of decking needed replacing, 600 square feet of ceiling had to be burned and repainted, ten wooden columns would have to be replaced, and box beams would have to be patched, burned, and repainted. A tin roof over the whole thing would have to be scraped and repainted with "roofer's red," a paint formulated to protect metal roofs. At least the tin was intact and, although the paint was worn, there were no holes in the roof. The steps from the sidewalk and stringers (the saw-toothed boards that support the steps), as it turned out, would have to be replaced completely.

"I bought a heavy-duty crowbar and heavy gloves and began to rip up the creaky old tongue-and-groove," Allan says. Next thing I knew, I had a growing pile of splintered trash in the side yard. I had the foresight to remove all the nails from the boards before I threw them on the pile. I was thinking of myself, primarily, and how a punctured palm could ruin a whole day. Only then did I think ahead to the safety of whoever would remove the pile of trash from my side yard." He had to bribe the city trash men to take the mess away.

At one point, Allan decided that the work was beyond him and hired a contractor recommended by neighbors who used per diem laborers. They removed the rotten columns and easily put the new ones in place.

All that remained was stripping 80 years of paint before repainting. The day laborer hired for the job started into stripping with a heat gun. While Allan's wife was on an errand, a spark from the heat gun started a fire that quickly spread to the interior of the porch. The laborer high-tailed it to parts unknown, stopping briefly at the nearby fire station to report the blaze.

"The good news is they saved my house," Allan said. "The bad news is it took me another month and several hundred dollars to repair the damage they did to the porch roof. That repair project was one I did myself."

The lesson Allan learned from his Victorian-porch fiasco is simple, and you can see it in the front porch on his present home. The porch is all of 20 square feet. It has no roof. And every inch of it is concrete.

---

6. JUST BECAUSE IT'S NEW

Even McMansions will need a little work.

■ ■ ■

Although renovations are usually associated with older houses, buyers of new homes may face challenges, too.

A lot of people buy a new house so they don't have to worry about renovation projects. Now, it's true that renovating a fixer-upper might be more costly over time than buying new, but new houses are hardly maintenance free. Too often, buyers of new houses believe that, just because the house is new, all they have to do is move in, close the front door, turn on the TV, and sign the checks for the mortgage each month.

That's not the way it is, says Gary G. Schaal, "the Guru of New," who has sold new houses to thousands of buyers since 1973. He says many new buyers begin making changes to their houses right from the start, trying to personalize them. He admits that a lot of new-home buyers think the house will take care of itself, but that attitude doesn't last very long. Unfortunately, however, they tend to blame the builder for everything, especially the things that they, just like any homeowner, should be taking care of.

Although most new houses don't require the kind of mainte-nance that older houses need, new houses do need care. Without a road map, many buyers neglect tasks and, as a result, encounter un-necessary problems. For example, a homeowner needs to drain the outdoor faucet and disconnect the hose before freezing weather sets in, even if they shut off the water. If that procedure isn't followed and the faucet is damaged or freezes, it's the homeowner's problem, even if the faucet is billed as frost free. *Frost free* doesn't mean maintenance free.

Wet basements often appear in new houses as well as old ones. Wet basements may result from buyers regrading the basement perimeter for landscaping, causing the water from rain and melting snow to flow toward, rather than away, from the house. Gary Schaal says that wet basements caused by the owner aren't covered in typical new-house warranties, so the homeowner has to take care of the problem at their own expense. A basement-perimeter drainage system often will run the homeowner $2,500 to $6,000, while property regrading can cost more than $5,000.

Before we go on, let's talk about home warranties. Many states require new-home builders to provide warranties. Most new houses come with ten-year warranties designed to help ease the financial burden of such calamities and protect builders from lawsuits. In some states, if the builder can't afford to offer one, an insurance pool provides it. Even with such warranties, new-home buyers need to check the reputation of the builders they are dealing with, visit other communities they have built, and check with residents there.

A new-home warranty covers mechanicals—plumbing, electricity, and heating and cooling—for the first two years. As the years pass, fewer things are covered, although the structure itself is guaranteed for the life of the warranty. If the builder isn't around at the end, the warranty provider picks up the tab. But it isn't perpetual care. If something happens 15 or 20 years down the road, it isn't going to be covered, Gary says.

In recent years, warranties have been available for older homes. The first year is often paid for by the seller or the seller's agent and usually has no cost limit on the problems it covers. This policy can be renewed annually for as long as the buyer wants to pay about $400 a year. These warranties usually have a $50 deductible for each occurrence, so if your furnace, toilet, and kitchen sink go at the same time, you are immediately out $150. These warranties also don't cover outside pipes, such as sewer lines, or roofs.

Despite the perception that people buy new houses because they refuse to become willing victims of the stress of renovating, it is not true, as Gary Schaal points out. Folks who buy new homes are willing to spend thousands within the first few years to finish off space such as bonus rooms, attics, and basements. The National Association of Home Builders reports that new-home buyers typically spend $6,475 on improvements during the first year of homeownership, usually on landscaping, decks, patios, and driveways.

The one advantage that owners of new homes have over most owners of older homes is that usually no surprises behind the walls have to be tackled before renovation can begin. They can expect fast gratification with few worries about something else going wrong that will make spending all that money look like the wrong decision.

Things do go wrong in a new house, however, and anyone who tries to offer you a guarantee that they won't is either a liar or a fool, or both, Schaal says. There are two reasons for such deficiencies, and both provide some insight into why any job can have a problem. The first reason is that the subcontractor caused it while doing the work. The second is caused by material movement, which is natural. Materials do settle, so you'll have that popped nail, the crack over the archway, or bowed floor joists.

Most builders will readily acknowledge that shrinkage of materials is more prevalent than it was 40 years ago, because building procedures have changed drastically. Thanks to vapor barriers, tighter sheathing, insulation, weather stripping, and caulking, today's house is almost airtight. Therefore, shrinkage, and the cracks and problems such as uneven flooring that result, is more intense.

What you need to do is try to reduce that intensity. One way is to buy a humidifier, which introduces some moisture into a dry, tight house. Another way is to avoid overheating the house in the winter, which will dry out a tight house even more. Open the windows periodically, even on cold days. Winter heating can even change the moisture content of the wood, temporarily warping interior slab and bifold doors. The solution is simple and involves applying wax to the tracks of the bifolds to stop the doors from sticking. Raised-panel wood doors can shrink or expand at times, revealing unfinished surfaces. It's a maintenance, rather than a warranty, issue.

Areas of painted walls often vary in color and texture, the result of touching up in the finishing process of the house. This is acceptable under warranty, as is color variation of stains on woodwork. Resilient (vinyl) floors in high-moisture areas, such as bathrooms, sometimes show raised nail heads because of joist movement, and although builders use adhesives to keep nails to a minimum, this technique doesn't always work. You can redrive the nails using a block of wood and a hammer.

Ridges often appear where a vinyl floor meets the edge of a toilet or bathroom. This is caused by water seeping into adhesive through a seam after installation. These areas should be periodically caulked with an acrylic designed for use in bathrooms.

Ceramic, marble, slate, and quarry tile floors can be damaged by heavy objects. Cracks that develop in the grout can be repaired with premixed grout from a home center, which typically comes in a color that matches. Joints can shrink where the ceramic tile meets the bathtub or shower area. Periodic caulking is required.

Carpeting can come loose because of an increase in humidity. Professional cleaning is recommended, and conventional shampooing is preferred over steam cleaning, because there is always a chance of permanent damage to the pile.

A lot of other issues can arise. These days, new-home builders are providing comprehensive manuals to buyers, which list all the problems that can arise and how to handle them as well as regular maintenance issues. The problem is, according to Gary, that most buyers don't bother to read the manual. In fact, once they are in the house, they can't even remember where they put it.

When you, as the owner of a new home, embark upon a home-improvement project, you will need a permit. The permit the builder obtained to construct your house doesn't extend past the day you take possession of it. Any project you undertake, whether finishing the basement or building a deck, may need a permit, so check with your local municipal building department before you start. Otherwise, the fines could end up costing you more than the project you planned to tackle.

One point of conflict in new homes and remodeling jobs is when the work is supposed to be finished. In outdoor work, such as a installing a deck or replacing a roof, delays are caused by the weather. A major source of delays in indoor and outdoor renovation jobs is the addition of work, either because the homeowner changes their mind about what they want or because of a problem uncovered during construction. Very few disputes involving construction end up in court, in part because of the high cost of prolonged litigation but mostly because the issues involved frequently aren't earth shattering. When you add up the cost of litigation and compare it with the cost of the problem, then unless the builder has really screwed up, there's really no point in going to court. These days, most of the bigger disputes go to mediation conducted by a growing number of mediation services firms. The goal is not to let things get so out of hand that you need a mediator to solve the problem for you.

7. HOW MUCH SHOULD YOU DO?

Some people are handy; the rest should let others do the work.

■ ■ ■

A group of Jim Remsen's friends and neighbors have gathered in his backyard this warm, mid-August evening, listening to a trio of folk musicians from Connecticut. The musicians are performing their music on a raised patio of flagstones under a huge pine tree. The flagstones continue for several feet in either direction, creating a large and attractive surface for entertaining or for simple summer meals. Jim can do little about the mosquitoes other than provide bug spray, but the atmosphere created by the patio, the landscaping, and the folk music contribute to an enjoyable time.

The flagstone patio was a family project involving Jim and two of his sons. It included a 300-mile roundtrip journey to a stone quarry in central Pennsylvania, where Jim and his older son loaded tons of flagstone onto a rented truck and hauled it back home.

Jim Remsen embarked on a project normally handled by a landscape architect or contractor and a crew with a backhoe. Some might consider this endeavor perfectly natural, yet others might consider it foolhardy. After I take you through the basics of Jim's project and those of others, some of you doubters are more than likely to change your minds and begin considering remodeling projects that you can do yourself.

There are only two reasons why you should ever take on a project that is usually best left to professionals. The first reason is, obviously, financial. If you can prove to yourself beyond any doubt that doing the project yourself will save you a substantial amount of money, then proceed. Saving money is not limited to materials costs. You need to factor in the amount of time that you will spend on the project from beginning to end. Your time is valuable. Would it, perhaps, be better to spend a few days working overtime to pay a professional, especially if that professional can do the job in a few days, rather than devote two or three months of nights and weekends, away from your job and family, to the job?

Here is the second, and what I consider the better, reason for doing it yourself. Carefully study and research all the aspects of what you wish to have done, including interviewing professionals and people who have done similar projects. After weighing all of the evidence, if you decide that you can do the job better than any professional, then do it yourself.

The corollary to this rule is that if there's no one willing or able to do the work that you want, you will have to do it yourself. Otherwise, the project will never get done.

In Jim Remsen's case, rules one and two apply. By driving to central Pennsylvania and buying the flagstone at the quarry, his materials cost was a third of what it would have been had he bought the stone from a retailer in his area, even when you factor in the cost of the one-way rental of a truck.

Once the flagstone was home, problems with the site had to be handled that no plan, no matter how detailed, could have accommodated. For example, the original plan contained nothing about the raised patio that the musicians used as a stage.

"When we dug the base for the patio, we found that the large pine tree that shaded it had roots going everywhere," Jim said. "We needed to cut the roots back and dig around them, and when we couldn't take care of all of them without killing the tree, we raised the patio to accommodate it. I don't think anyone we could have hired would have been able to do the job we did, and even if they could have done it, the price would have skyrocketed."

The toughest part of the job had nothing to do with the actual work. "The truck had a rearview mirror that was broken, but I didn't find it out until I was well under way," Jim said. "I had to stop every few miles to fix it. Otherwise, I was driving blind."

Experience is a great teacher, but if you have no experience, the best way to get some is to plan carefully, learn as much as you can, swallow hard, and then take the leap.

Vic Gatmaitan and Melissa Rooney have a large, second-floor front room with bay windows. They thought it would make a perfect family room—something that older houses don't typically have. They also thought that it needed something to set it apart from the other rooms of the house, and, after watching one or another home improvement TV show, decided on a metal ceiling.

Metal ceilings were very popular from the early 1900s through the 1930s, more in commercial applications than residential. They were an interesting alternative to plaster. There were dozens of manufacturers, and installation was part of the repertoire of just about any carpenter.

Once something goes out of fashion, especially for so long, both the materials and the people who work with them follow suit. Fewer than a dozen metal ceiling manufacturers are in business today, and perhaps one in a thousand carpenters has heard of them, let alone installed them. Still, when old-house owners rediscover metal ceilings, interest in them regenerates. They gained some popularity among the so-called urban pioneers of the 1970s, again in the late 1980s after they were featured in a *This Old House* segment, and in the late 1990s after another TV appearance and when Home Depot began selling them at some outlets.

Undeterred, Vic and Melissa, relatively new to do-it-yourself projects, examined all the options and decided that the metal ceiling was a job they could handle. They bought the materials and read and reread the detailed instructions until they thought they were ready. They borrowed tools from neighbors to cut the plywood that had to go on the ceiling before the ceiling plates, affixed to the plywood with tiny aluminum nails, could be installed.

Standing on stepladders, they found the center of the ceiling and snapped chalk lines so that all the plates that needed to be cut to fit were at the edges of the ceiling where the cuts could be hidden by metal trim.

Because they had decided not to paint the ceiling, cutting the trim to fit seamlessly was critical, because errors could not be hidden with oil-based caulk. (Latex caulk and paint rust metal.) This was a huge challenge for Melissa, because even wood trim is not that easy to cut and fit if you've never done it before, and I've known many carpenters who rely heavily on caulk and wood filler.

Her solution was to build a miter box of her own design and use a borrowed reciprocating saw—typically used to demolish rather than build—to cut the trim to fit. Her solution was perfect. It was based on the experience that she and Vic had gained in the earlier stages of the project and her growing confidence in her abilities.

"Our friends and family thought we were crazy," said Melissa, acknowledging that the job from start to finish swallowed up a couple of months of weekends and most evenings after work. "But once we were finished and they saw what we had done, they started asking us to install similar ceilings in their houses."

The answer was no.

The chief ingredient of a do-it-yourself project is confidence. A colleague of mine at the Danbury (Connecticut) *News-Times* in the early 1970s decided that he wanted to learn to sail small boats. He borrowed every sailing book in the public library and spent days and weekends interviewing boat owners and builders along the Connecticut shoreline. After about a year, he felt confident enough in his knowledge to buy a small, used sailboat. He then applied everything he had learned and been told and headed out a couple of miles into Long Island Sound, taking me along for the ride (I had brought the beer).

When we returned to the dock, the boat owners at the neighboring slips were cheering and applauding. My colleague continued to apply that confidence to other endeavors, such as building his own house and learning to fly small planes.

Success can be a great confidence builder if you remember rules one and two and the corollary to rule two. Unfortunately, we are only human and are bound to make mistakes, no matter how smart we think we are. For example, you should never undertake more than one major project at a time. And—and this extremely important—you should never take shortcuts, no matter how desperate you are to get the job done.

I had a bathroom on the third floor of my second house that was in dire need of work. Its cast-iron, claw-foot tub was large and inviting compared with the undersized one on the second floor, but it didn't drain quickly. The third-floor bath also held an ancient, leaky sink; a running toilet; and the expansion tank for the closed, hot-water heating system. It also had a dirty linoleum floor with sock-snagging nails that kept popping up.

It would need updated lighting and electrical outlets, a new sink and toilet, and a camp shower attachment to the tub. There would be wainscoting, new molding, a wooden radiator cover, and a tile floor to install.

I began obtaining estimates. The tile floor alone would cost $1,400 with labor and materials. No tile person would do the job unless the cast-iron tub was removed, and that was impossible. In addition, removing the linoleum, including all the little nails, was not even in the estimate.

The projected cost: $12,000. So I did it all myself. It took two years. When I was finished and calculated the costs, including my time, I had a $22,264.50 bathroom that was very nice but certainly not worth the money. In addition, the anecdotes surrounding that job, such as the Sunday night I put a nail through the hot-water line and found that the shutoff valve to the bathroom in the basement was rusted, and how the rat found its way into the house through the toilet drain that was open for several months, would fill another book.

When we decided to add a tub to the master bath of our present house, we hired a contractor. The job, which was as complicated as the third-floor bathroom project that I tackled, cost $14,000 but took only a few weeks. Every problem that arose was handled quickly.

The bottom line: Some jobs you can do, and some are better left to others. Be absolutely sure that you have the time, the ability, and the confidence to take on a renovation project and achieve a result that is both cost-effective and something you can be proud of.

8. IT'S NEVER AS EASY AS IT LOOKS

Despite what you see on TV, not everything is possible.

■ ■ ■

A few years ago, I had breakfast with Bob Vila during the International Builders Show. Before I left for the show, I told a friend of mine about the breakfast meeting. Her eyes narrowed. "You tell him that it's never as easy as he makes it look," urged my friend, who had been working on her house with her husband for too many years, I guess.

Because Bob has a huge audience and is synonymous with home improvement, I'm sure he takes lots of flak as well as praise. So I decided not to pass along my friend's criticism. But she is right. Television, by presenting life in sound bites, creates a false picture of home improvement. Shelter magazines, too, do their share. But television continues to have the greatest impact on how we spend our renovation dollars.

In the movie *Radio Days,* the boy who is supposed to be Woody Allen as a child breaks into a container he and friends had been using to collect money for his synagogue to buy a "secret decoder ring" advertised on the radio. In the rabbi's study with his parents, the boy hears the rabbi lecture his parents about how radio creates false hopes and dreams among impressionable youngsters. When the boy responds, "You are correct, my faithful Indian companion," the rabbi and his parents take turns slapping him.

I'd find myself wishing I could do the same to the TV home improvement people who make it all look so easy and unstressful.

I should slap myself a couple of times, because I've committed that sin. For three seasons, I was the Gadgeteer on the Discovery Channel's *Home Matters* program, which is now in reruns. For my first segment, I demonstrated how to rewire your telephone network box to add a dedicated line for a computer modem. For the sake of television, a somewhat complicated, daylong job for the average person had to be squeezed into four minutes.

In the next few days, I received 1,800 e-mails from people all over the country who had seen the segment but still couldn't figure out exactly how to do it. I sat down, wrote out a complete set of instructions, and e-mailed it 1,800 times.

Another time, I demonstrated how to clean and waterproof a pressure-treated deck, an annual maintenance job I absolutely hate. I did it in four minutes, about a minute less than they suggest the mildew remover needs to begin doing its work. When I had a deck, I typically spent a week cleaning and waterproofing it, looking over my shoulder, trying to keep ahead of the weather. But the impression I gave in both cases would lead you to believe that these jobs could be done in four minutes with your eyes closed.

I once spent a day in Norm Abram's *New Yankee Workshop.* Among the things I learned is that Norm starts projects but a guy named Hugh Kelly finishes them. Otherwise, they could never get the show done.

Another time, I spent a day on the set of *This Old House*'s Tucson, Arizona, project. As I stepped out of my rental car, I knew immediately that this wasn't real life when five subcontractors arrived as well. That only happens on TV. The show's producers demand high levels of craftsmanship, cutting-edge techniques, and the latest technology to keep *This Old House* a head or two above the competition. They get it, of course, and that's where this show differs from real life.

You and I plead with the plumber to show up on time. Master plumber Rich Trethewey snaps his fingers at 1:30 PM and the air-conditioning contractor appears. The owner of the house, an architect, talked Tucson's premier plasterer into coming out of retirement to stucco the outside and replaster the inside. The rest of America is running behind a Florida-bound Winnebago, yelling to the plasterer that age 95 is too young to throw in the towel.

On occasion, the rest of the country gets a fleeting glimpse of reality. One *This Old House* program took viewers behind the scenes, where they learned that economy was sacrificed if it wasn't "good television." In other words, instead of showing us ways to save money, we are shown how to spend more than the typical viewer could ever afford on things the typical viewer would never dream of owning.

Hometime has taken us once or twice in the last several years behind the scenes, but each time, it was more like "TV's Bloopers and Practical Jokes," with host Dean Johnson hitting his thumb with a hammer while on a roof and the various shortcomings of his cohosts being chronicled. One thing I can say for *Hometime* is that its project tapes, which are available from PBS or at home centers, are great teachers. I learned to tile successfully from one of those tapes, well enough, in fact, to tile not only my bathroom floor but my picky architect brother-in-law's as well. So well, in fact, that the other contractors on the job thought I was a professional.

I did have to watch the tape 200 times, however.

Some jobs do go quickly if you are used to doing them. But nothing goes according to plan, no matter how carefully you plan.

For example, the TV show demonstrates how to replace a sash cord or chain to get a window to move up and down again. It doesn't tell you that the window stop may crack when you remove it with a pry bar to get at the sash cord and weight. Nor does it suggest that the paint on the window may be lead-based, and when you get the window moving up and down again, lead dust may be produced as the window rubs against the side jambs.

A better approach, of course, would be to analyze the condition of each window. Should it be repaired or replaced? If it should be repaired, shouldn't you replace and reglaze the glass after stripping the paint from everything including the frame, then find a way to insulate the window frame for greater energy efficiency?

It takes about two days per window. I know. I did 31 of them in my old house. A better idea would be to install a sash replacement kit, which uses the original window jambs so you don't have to mess with the trim or inside and outside walls. You take out the old window stops (which crack no matter what) and install vinyl jamb liners and wood or vinyl sashes, creating a new, energy-efficient window.

I'm a great believer in recycling old materials. But getting old doors, molding, radiators, or mantelpieces ready for reuse is both time consuming and labor intensive.

Say you need to replace a door. The old opening is 32 by 84 inches, but standard doors, thanks to modern code, are 36 inches by 80 inches. The expensive solution is to order a custom-made door, costing up to $1,000. The inexpensive solution is to pick up a used door from a salvage yard for $10, but the used door has to be stripped, sanded, and refinished. The hardware has to be replaced, and because you can't find it in the home center, it has to be specially ordered. Old doors are often warped, and openings are usually out of plumb, and a lot of carpentry will be needed to get the door operating properly.

The total cost of the replacement door might be $100, but how much is your time worth? If you make $40 an hour at your regular job, the amount of time you spend working on one door may approach the cost of a custom door.

How valuable is your time? And is the satisfaction you get doing the job enough compensation?

The bottom line: It's never as easy as it looks. My friend, and Bob Vila, could tell you that.

---

9. IT NEVER ENDS . . . WELL, ALMOST NEVER

The light at the end of the tunnel will probably burn out.

■ ■ ■

If Matt Schultz could do it over again, "I would have told the previous owner to bring the house up to code."

"That way I wouldn't have had to wait so long to get to the fun stuff," said Matt, who lives with wife Judie and daughter Helen, in a 3,200-square-foot, 1892 Queen Anne–style house in Lansdowne, Pennsylvania, a Philadelphia suburb. Matt, who bought the house from a friend shortly after graduating from college in 1988, acknowledged that, "I underestimated the amount of work. But I was young and eager, and I convinced myself that I could do it."

The house had most of its original architecture, which was a plus for Matt, a preservationist and, today, the executive director of the Philadelphia Society for the Preservation of Landmarks. It also was affordable, because he convinced the owner to take back the mortgage. He and Judie were engaged and a year away from their wedding day, but she was on board with the decision to buy the house and jumped in with both feet.

"A friend of ours said she had seen a segment on a talk show that urged couples to build a piece of furniture before they get married to see how well they can work together," said Matt. "During the year we worked on the house before we were married, we developed a deep understanding of one another as well as the meaning of teamwork and how it can accomplish so much."

With a lot of house to redo, where did they start? "We decided to start on the third floor, to create a space that was freshly painted and would reflect what the rest of the house would look like when it was finished," he said.

So on a Labor Day weekend with temperatures hovering in the 90s, he and Judie rented wallpaper steamers and began stripping the walls. The steamers, working in concert, drew enough juice to keep blowing out fuses in the antiquated electrical system. "We sat at the top of the third floor stairs and kept asking ourselves why we were doing this," Schultz said. "We laugh about it now, but it wasn't as funny 16 years ago."

What they should have done first was hire an electrician to bring the service up to code and replace the fuses with circuit breakers. "We also decided to call a guy and pay him to scrape all the walls in the house," Schultz said. "By the end of a single day, the guy had done the entire house, and the wallpaper he removed was sitting in plastic bags on our front porch waiting for disposal."

Rather than renovation per se—although upgrading electrical work and plumbing to modern standards does count as renovation—the Schultzes have spent the last 16 years "restoring" their Victorian house. "It was so much more difficult and involved than I thought it would be, and certainly more expensive," Matt said, "but it certainly was real confidence builder."

For the first dozen years, Schultz would devote an hour a day to the house after work, even if it were something as seemingly inconsequential as touch-up painting. "I would daydream at work about what I was going to do on the house at night and on the weekends," he said.

The jobs included building a first-floor powder room (half-bath), restoring the second-floor bathroom to its original look—a job so well-executed that it was the subject of an article in *Old House Journal*—redoing all the plumbing and electrical work, removing all the lead paint and asbestos, repainting the house inside and out, refinishing the floors, and restoring all the windows and doors. Each of the two dozen windows had been painted shut. Each had to be opened, stripped of lead-based paint, reglazed, and then repainted.

"The nastiest job was sanding the floors," Matt said. "It was a hot day, and I was covered from head to toe with dust. Everything, including me, smelled of the varnish I'd just sanded from the floor. Most of the house gets dirty, so if you buy a house and plan to refinish the floors, have it done before you move in."

The Schultzes decided to have all the lead-based paint and asbestos removed from the house long before they were ready to have children. "In fact, the major work on the house was done before Helen was born," he said. "Not only can the work be harmful to a child's health, but children limit the amount of time you can spend on the house and certainly redirect your financial resources." Once they knew Helen, now ten, was on the way, "We were motivated to do the work and accelerated the schedule."

These days, with the house pretty much in order after completing a bathroom on the third floor, Schultz now spends a half-hour each night pulling weeds out of the garden, which the couple also created. "We are down to managing things instead of having to rebuild and replace."

"Working on a house can be therapeutic," Matt said. "One of the things the house did for me was to keep the creative juices flowing. My career has had its ups and downs, but the house has always been there for me, providing me with something I can be passionate about." That passion has helped the Schultzes "write our own chapter of the history of this house."

"I was joking the other day about moving, and Helen immediately objected," Matt said. "She argued, and correctly so, that 'none of my friends have a house that is anything like this one.'"

"We've created a product that our family and friends can enjoy." Matt has thrown himself into volunteer work in his hometown, including the restoration of the early 20th-century train station and preservation of war memorials, among other projects. "When you enter the front door, it is just like being in a time warp to a different era," he said. "We achieved our vision. And we'd do it again in a second."

10. BIGGER ISN'T ALWAYS BETTER

A little creativity can go a long way—and save lots of money.

■ ■ ■

When they were first married 28 years ago, Lane and Denise Cavalieri Fike bought what they could afford: a 12-foot-wide, 5-room, brick house built in 1835 for $50,000. Two sons and several large dogs later, the Fikes are still in that house, although it has undergone several transformations in those nearly three decades. The fruit of their many labors is likely worth more than the $400,000 median price of comparable but grander houses in their neighborhood.

Despite all the changes, the house is no larger than when the couple started, proving that if you are creative and make the most of what you have, you don't have to get bigger to be better. The compactness of the house has always contributed to a feeling of family for the Fikes. "I liked the fact that such a little house always made us close, Denise said. "We were always here together. But the boys were always able to go off into their room and be alone just by shutting the door."

It's fortunate, too, that Lane is an engineer and Denise is an artist and designer known for her hand-painted wallpaper that graces the walls of many of the nation's children's hospitals. This means that Lane and Denise have been able to play off each other's substantial talents over the years to transform their small house into a workable and comfortable home for themselves and their sons, Hunter, 22, and Tyler, 19. They've created a house that looks much larger than its 1,200 square feet. Considering the typical new American home is 2,300 square feet, according to the National Association of Homebuilders, this is no small feat. Theirs is just a small footprint, one so small that nothing fits up the narrow, spiral staircase.

When they first moved in, Lane designed and built the bed for their third-floor bedroom, cutting the pieces in the basement and assembling it in the room. He also built a Shaker-style armoire with lots of storage space to make up for the shortage of closets.

Getting the mattress up to the third floor wasn't easy. Anything big in a small house has to go through the window. "We attached the mattress to a rope," Denise said. "I climbed out the third-floor window to the second-floor roof. Lane stood in the garden and was pushing it up. I told Lane I couldn't hold it anymore. Just then, a man came bounding over the rooftops, pulled the mattress up, pushed it through the window, and disappeared."

"We never saw him again," Denise said.

One thing about a small house is that you don't need a lot of furniture. There's no place to put it. "In a small house, you put one or two things down, and it looks messy," Denise said. "If you lay a coat down in a big house, it looks like a coat. If you put a coat down in a small house, it looks like a piece of furniture."

When the boys were ready to leave the crib, they moved directly to bunk beds in a second-floor room. Lane bought two plain beds and built a frame around them, adding a fireman's pole, a chin-up pole, and a removable slide from the top bunk, with shelves and desk attached. The desk could be easily converted to what Denise called "Fort Fike," a fortress-like structure the boys could play in. Lane also created built-in drawers for the boys' clothes.

In the kitchen, Lane has built all sorts of hideaway storage and cutting boards. They replaced a small window in the back with sliding glass doors to the back garden, allowing them to close off a side door that had been the access to the back. In that tiny but well-organized kitchen, Denise runs a side business, producing cannoli, an Italian dessert, for local stores and restaurants.

They landscaped the garden, with Lane designing and building a fountain and pool. In the summer, they set up a collapsible table that Lane made and entertained their friends there.

What they really needed was a family room. Though not big TV watchers, the Fikes spent many years crowding the third-floor bedroom when they did watch a show, because there's no place in the 12-by-12 living room for a television. To solve the problem, Denise rented space and freed the second-floor room she'd always used as her studio to be a family room. The only space they regret not having is a dining room. They continue to eat in the kitchen, at a drop-leaf table.

The latest renovation effort brought them recognition from *Better Homes and Gardens,* which gave the Fikes's bathroom remodeling project an award of merit and a check for $100—not enough to make a dent in the project cost of about $6,000 (bids were as high as $25,000) but still pretty respectable for transforming the 3-by-6 room into something Denise calls the "Taj Mahal" when she compares it to the space she replaced.

This was not the first bathroom redo. The last one was 18 years before, and Denise changes the color scheme and repaints the room every three or four years. But the 4½-foot tub was small and ugly, and she couldn't stand it.

As with many renovation projects, however, the impetus for a new bathroom was a problem. "I looked up at the living room ceiling and saw a small stain. We traced it to the bathtub. As the leak got worse, the stain started getting bigger, so Lane and I decided that this might be a good time to redo the bathroom. The bathroom is the only one they have, which meant that to do anything to it at all, they'd need to stay in a hotel during the work. That added up only to four nights during the two weeks of construction, because the plumbing was reconnected and the bathroom was usable.

They had to redo the living room ceiling as well. Denise Fike had papered the plaster ceiling for 20-minute segment on HGTV's *Design Basics.* Now she replaced the paper with copper leaf.

The contractor actually removed a corner of the bathroom to increase the square footage. That helped accommodate a new tub—the smallest Jacuzzi the company makes—but it still had to be brought through the bathroom window, and a corner cabinet had to be removed to get it inside.

Denise first chose some inexpensive tile, but when her friends said that tile "wasn't her," she went with pale-blue polished slate—12-by-12-inch with "zero grout, because I'm tired of mold." Rounding out the renovation were glass doors along the tub for the shower; a low-flow, low-profile toilet from France called a porché; a 10-inch green porcelain sink with a gray granite top; high-hat lighting; Belgian Arte wallpaper, and space-saving cabinets. While the room was not the bathroom of her dreams, she at least had a chance to luxuriate in a tub that wasn't in a hotel for the first time in 28 years.

The Fikes haven't even considered moving since 1985, when Tyler was born, but Lane acknowledges that living in a small house has the occasional drawback, especially since Denise is forever redecorating. "She once temporarily stored something on the stairs to the basement," he said. "I didn't see it, tripped, fell down the stairs, and broke both my legs."

11. MIND THE NEIGHBORS

Bricks and mortar aren't the only way to build walls.

■ ■ ■

A friend of mine looked out the window of her house one late autumn morning to discover that the neighboring residence was undergoing renovation.

That was the good news. Rehabilitation of dilapidated housing in city neighborhoods is a good sign and generally means rising property values with the resulting improvement to the quality of life, including increased security. The bad news was that the remodeling contractor had knocked a hole in the wall separating the two houses to permit him to run an electrical line from the street to power his tools and light his work area—without informing my friend or other neighbors.

Only when pressed did the contractor agree to repair the wall once the project was completed and to close the opening with a sheet of plywood when no work was being done. He didn't do so immediately, however, and a series of other affronts to my friend and her neighbors created much ill will. The stress that my friend endured during the course of the project was not worth the end result. And just think of the testy atmosphere into which the property's owner will move once the house is finished!

Sometimes the work being done ends up being more disruptive to your neighbors than you ever imagined.

Vic Gatmaitan and Melissa Rooney wanted the wood floors of their duplex sanded and refinished. To avoid the inconvenience and the sawdust and odor of the polyurethane used to seal and protect the sanded floors, the couple went to New Mexico for a few days while the work was being done. It never occurred to them to tell the neighbors on the other side of the party wall. The odor of the oil-based polyurethane filled the neighbors' home, seeping through spaces where the floors and walls meet that had opened as the century-old house settled.

When the neighbors came over to complain, the refinishers told them they could do nothing about the odor and to just open the windows. It was midwinter, and the nighttime temperature hovered at 20 degrees. The neighbors opened the windows and cranked the furnace thermostat to 80. Fortunately, the neighbors had done their share of renovation, including refinishing floors. Any ill will was directed against the floor refinishing crew, who should have known all the risks.

The refinishers were the low bidders. You get what you pay for.

Unless you live on a mountaintop in the middle of nowhere, any change you make to your house will somehow affect your neighbors. Say you are having your front porch repainted. The color may not be an issue, especially if it is white or some neutral color that fits well into the rest of the neighborhood. The work itself can lead to ill will, however. Issues can include where the painter parks his truck, what time the painting crew starts and ends its work, the dust and noise created by scraping and sanding loose paint, the odor of paint being burned off surfaces with an acetylene torch, and environmental issues created by the residue, especially if the paint being removed is lead-based. Then there is the noise—especially of the radio that most work crews can't seem to do without.

The issues involved grow with the scope of the project, especially if it is a major addition requiring planning and zoning action that is dependent on the neighbors' concurrence. A California developer once observed that when neighbors appear en masse at a hearing on your project, the battle is over already and you've lost it. Even after neighbors have agreed to put up with the disruption that your project will cause, you've got to protect their interests from start to finish.

That's what Alex and Beth Cerrato tried to do for Scott and Allison Leverick, the neighbors most affected by their six-month addition. "The project was going to require removing the grass and shrubs two feet into the Levericks' yard," Alex said. "So we talked to them well before the work began, and they agreed to it, as long as what was removed was replaced." Instead of grass seed, the lawn was to be replaced with more expensive sod. The shrubs that had to be relocated would be returned and, in very clear terms, no trucks were to be parked on the Levericks' front lawn.

About midway through the project, Alex's grandfather died. Alex, Beth, and their son, Ben, left town for the funeral. While they were away, a subcontractor, although cognizant of the parking ban, allowed the truck delivering drywall to drive onto the Levericks' lawn, damaging a section of sidewalk and several feet of grass and causing cracks to appear in their foundation wall.

Not only did the apologetic contractor fix the walk and replace the ruined grass with sod, he repaired a crack in the Levericks' foundation that may or may not have been caused by the work and gave them tickets to a baseball game. Impressed, Scott Leverick hired one of the subcontractors to handle some work on his house. "And Scott never hires anyone," said Allison of her do-it-yourself husband.

"They're not only our neighbors but our friends," Beth said. "We weren't going to let anything affect our friendship."

On the other hand, little can be done with a neighbor who will view everything you do with suspicion and go out of the way to promote confrontation. To ensure that your project is successful and to minimize conflict, you'll need to clue in the contractor well before the contract is signed and make absolutely certain that all of his workers and subcontractors are aware of the neighbor problem. And it is up to you, as the person who pays the bills, to make sure that the contractor enforces the rules and is the one who apologizes to your neighbors for any infractions. Even if the contractor is in the right, they'll have to accept any blame to keep the peace and get the job done.

In most situations, however, familiarity doesn't breed contempt. If my friend and her neighbors had gotten to know the person employing the contractor, they could have brought their concerns about the contractor to the owner and reduced ill will. Instead, they confronted someone whose chief concern was getting the job done on time. A better contractor would have notified the employer immediately of the neighbors' concerns and tried to bring the two sides together. Or the contractor would have gone out of his or her way to address the neighbors' complaints as soon as possible.

It may seem like extra work for no pay, but it makes great business sense. After all, wouldn't you rather hire someone whose work you know than a stranger?

12. DON'T RENOVATE TO SELL

Second-guessing the next owner can cost you.

■ ■ ■

It may have been greed or simply ignorance, but a seller once spent $60,000 for a new kitchen in the hope of making his already sellable house even more so. As Realtor Joanne Davidow tells the story, the buyer immediately gutted the kitchen after moving in. It was a lot of money spent for nothing.

Every year, *Remodeling* publishes its "Cost versus Value" survey, in which the magazine looks at popular renovation projects and how much of the cost of the particular project a homeowner can expect to recoup when the house is sold. The survey, which the magazine breaks down along regional lines, provides no guarantees. The point that *Remodeling* attempts to drive home is that, no matter what you do to your house, you shouldn't expect to get the money you spent back the next day.

You would not believe how many readers and professionals alike miss that point. Remember: No matter what renovation project you undertake, the goal should be to make living in your house easier and more comfortable for you and your family. If you are planning to sell somewhere down the road, however, you might want to consider how the renovation project will affect how quickly the house will sell and how much it will sell for.

For example, if everyone on your block has a deck and you don't, you might want to consider adding one. Or, if they all have decks, you might want to add a landscaped patio to attract those buyers who don't want the maintenance chores most decks require. I've had both, and prefer the patio.

If you want to spend your renovation money wisely and are looking to recoup your investment down the road when you sell, anything you do to your house will have to be done in context. What this means is that you'll need to look at the other houses on your street and see what makes them desirable or lacking—or repulsive.

The next step is to determine what's in style and what isn't. The answer may be no farther away than the model homes at new-home developments. Builders employ market research companies to determine trends, then hire architects and designers to create models that show off what's new and hot in a mouth-watering manner. The goal is to create "memory points" for the buyer, which, simply put, means that a buyer walks into a model home and is swept away by something they see. Even if the buyer sees 100 model houses at 25 new-home developments, the "memory" of some feature lingers and draws the person back to that model.

Of course, a couple visiting these houses may be attracted by different things. For instance, a wife may remember that the island in the kitchen had drawers big enough for large pots and pans, while a husband may have focused on the fact that the garage could be converted to a workshop.

The moral: Figure out which memory point ranks highest on your list and tackle that first. Then move on to the next one.

Unless you are rebuilding after a fire, don't load your plate with too many projects at once. Some people think that enduring massive dislocation for a little while is better than having to live through a series of upheavals. That argument seems valid. However, because you as the homeowner must maintain control of the renovation process at all times, doing one project at a time—or a couple of related projects—is the wiser course. You need to fight the urge for immediate gratification.

Now that you have an idea of what is hot, it's time to determine what's not, and that is a house in which maintenance has been deferred. High-end buyers avoid houses needing lots of work. At the same time, low-income and moderate-income people often don't have the resources to bring the house up from the depths. And, frankly, do you want to live in a house that only the Addams Family or the Munsters would find comfortable?

First, contact a real estate agent who focuses on your area and invite the agent over to chat and look at your house. Don't worry about the commission or making a commitment to the agent to sell your house when the time comes. If the agent is savvy and not short-sighted, they will use this first contact to expand knowledge of the neighborhood as well as develop a relationship with you. A good agent will know what is selling and what isn't, both now and over time. If having a deck is what buyers seem to want, then the agent will know, right down to the size and the kind of wood.

Ask the agent to recommend a couple of home inspectors, but here's a caveat: inspection companies have been pushing "preinspections" to people planning to put their houses on the market a few months down the road. The home inspector finds problems that could become issues during negotiations with the buyers and reduce the list price. This preinspection gives the buyer a chance to tackle them before the house goes up for sale.

A lot of real estate agents have problems with this concept, because the more a seller knows, the more the seller legally has to disclose. If the seller fails to disclose, the buyer will have more ammunition to take to court, but trying to second-guess buyers is not your real goal. Instead, you are trying to get a handle on problems before they occur. By getting the drop on problems, you can reduce the cost of repairs and try to find things that might bury a renovation project in extra work and higher costs.

For example, let's say you want to add a bathtub to the master bath. You realize that the ceiling below the bathtub will require reinforcement. What you don't know is that the water lines are not up to code and the drain lines aren't doing their job and water is stagnating in drain traps. An experienced home inspector will pick that up simply by smell and turning on the faucets. The inspector then will suggest bringing in an expert—in this case a plumber—to look further into the problem and offer solutions. The real estate agent should have a list of plumbers, roofers, and other contractors they recommend to sellers.

Although the inspector's job is not to establish priorities for you, the information that the inspector and other experts provide will be invaluable. Whatever you do, don't chisel your list of priorities in stone. The unexpected invariably happens, and you need to be flexible.

■ THINGS TO REMEMBER

1. Simple, inexpensive changes can personalize a house.

2. Use your home inspection report to establish priorities.

3. Consider doing major projects in phases to limit disruptions.

4. Try to make better use of what you have before you buy new.

5. Selling and moving is sometimes a better idea than staying and renovating.

6. Don't overenlarge. If you live in a three-bedroom neighborhood, a four-bedroom house probably won't sell for a premium.

7. Don't rush to renovate. Live in your house for a while before launching a major project.

8. Need more room? Get rid of clutter rather than renovate.

9. If you don't have the intestinal fortitude, don't buy a fixer-upper.

10. Expect something to go wrong. It always does.

11. Bad things can happen to new houses, even if you have a good builder.

12. Nothing is completely maintenance-free. A regular maintenance program will put a cap on problems.

13. Never take on more work than you can tackle in a reasonable time. Projects need a time limit.

14. Do projects that will not tax your abilities and will give you personal satisfaction, especially ones that few professionals are willing to undertake.

15. Never assume that what you see on television can be done easily in your house.

16. When you sign on to homeownership, it implies a long-term commitment. Never think that the last project will be the last one.

17. Try to have the worst jobs, such as refinishing the floors or removing hazardous materials, done before you move in.

18. Even the grunt work that people say you can do is often more cost-effective and quicker if you have a professional do it.

19. Be creative with the space you have.

20. Problems usually beget renovation projects.

21. Never launch a major renovation project without talking to the neighbors first.

22. Make sure your contractor and their subcontractors communicate with the neighbors as the project progresses.

23. Never argue. Have the contractor fix whatever they break on the neighbors' property.

24. Never embark on a major renovation project because you think it will raise the asking price for your house.

25. Tackle small projects that make the house you are selling look more appealing.

PART 2

ROLL UP YOUR SLEEVES

■ ■ ■

With all the complaints I hear from consumers about contractors, and vice versa, it was difficult for me to believe that I could find anyone who could make it through a six-month project and not be punching holes in new drywall. Yet, when I called to interview them, Alex and Beth Cerrato warned me that they might be the wrong couple to talk to, because they were completely happy with the work that created a 1,500-square-foot addition.

That's not been my experience. I can remember all the stray nails my 10-month-old found at the end of each day that the contractor and crew pronounced their work areas "broom clean." I also remember the number of bottles of antacid I consumed over the course of every job.

Most people have experiences more like mine than the Cerratos's. Theirs is the one we all want to have, the Rolls Royce of renovations, not the Yugo. It isn't that easy, because there are so many ducks to get in that row before we start—and so much bad advice that some of us are doomed from the start.

It is all in the plan. If your plan has cracks, so will your basement walls. It's all about good working relationships. If you start out not trusting your contractor, you will more than likely feel even worse about him or her by the end of the job.

So make sure all those ducks are in that row. Make sure your financing is in order. Make sure that the contract covers all your concerns. Insist that all the permits be in hand before the work starts. If the plan doesn't look workable, don't be afraid to change it. Just make sure you tell the contractor when you want to change things, reach an agreement, get the changes down in writing, and make sure you both sign off on everything.

Remember: The contractor is the lead duck. If he becomes lost, so will the rest of them. And your goose will be cooked.

13. THE PERFECT MATCH

You *can* be happy from the start of your renovation
till the day it ends.

■ ■ ■

Here's a renovation story with a happy beginning, middle, and end, which is as rare as snow in San Diego. What you are about to read is probably the gold standard. If you can come up with a renovation experience that even approaches this one, you're doing very well. And if you're a contractor, this, my friend, is the way you should do business.

Alex and Beth Cerrato survived a six-month renovation process that virtually doubled the size of their house, and they have no complaints. "After a while, you just get into a routine," said Beth, who acknowledged that being confined day-after-day, six days a week, to a 16-by-20 room with an 18-month-old for three of those six months can wear you down.

"When I needed to take a shower, the crew would stop work and leave the second floor for 20 minutes until I was finished," she said. "Ben goes down for his nap between 1:00 and 3:00 PM, so the subs needed to work in another part of the house until he was up again."

At one point, to get to the outside from the first floor, they had to go through the basement. "We ate dinner out a lot," she said. "Still, we could always see the light at the end of the tunnel," even as Thanksgiving passed and Christmas and the family dinner planned for that day loomed.

The project, a two-story addition to their 1,500-square-foot house, cost just about what they'd paid for the place six years earlier—$157,000. In return for their expenditure, they got the house they wanted that easily accommodates two adults and now two children, with the recent addition of another son, Colton.

"Resale was never a consideration in anything we did," said Alex, who quickly adds that he and Beth are planning to remain in the house for 30 years. That was not their intention when they bought the house. They assumed that they would move to something larger sooner. But when they began looking, they could find nothing under $500,000, and all of those houses also had three bedrooms and would need work, including central air conditioning.

"We could have moved to another town, but we like this one," Alex said, because of the school system. "We also like this block and our neighbors." Paying higher taxes was another big factor in the decision not to not spend $500,000 on a new house. "We didn't want to eat spaghetti forever," Beth said.

The couple had done some work on the house in the first six years they owned it. The floors were sanded and refinished, and the water problem in the basement was effectively managed with perimeter drains and a sump pump, so it could be finished off as a big-screen TV room and playroom for Ben.

What they wanted was more usable space. The kitchen was small and needed to be expanded. It had to be open to a family room, so Beth could keep an eye on the boys when she was cooking. They decided to get rid of the dining room in favor of an eat-in kitchen large enough to accommodate their families on holidays. They also made the family room open to the deck.

When the project was over, they had a master bedroom with a cathedral ceiling; a larger basement with an office for Alex; the kitchen, which opened into a family room that opened to a rebuilt deck; new siding; a new roof; larger storage areas; and a better looking front porch.

The project was massive, but what is notable about this job is how well Alex and Beth and their contractor "meshed." Long before they began calling contractors, they had an architect out to the house to look at what they wanted to do. A year went by while they got a plan in their heads. Alex and Beth called four or five contractors. The one they hired was recommended by the next-door neighbor. The contractor they chose wowed the couple from that first meeting. He was detail oriented, assured them without hesitation that they could have what they wanted, and even suggested trade-offs such as forgoing the double Jacuzzi tub in the master bath in favor of the basement addition. "He told us it wouldn't be fast, easy, or cheap," Alex said. "But he said it could be done."

Instead of hiring an architect for $5,000 to $7,000, they were provided with one by the contractor who did the job for $3,000. But even before the plans were on the drawing board, Alex and Beth had to receive formal education from the contractor. "There was an enormous amount of preliminary work before we even paid a penny," Alex said.

For two hours a week for ten weeks, Alex and Beth went to the contractor's office. The first session focused on architectural plans, another meeting was about windows, and another on lighting. There was a meeting with a molding specialist to talk about how to match existing molding and new. As their education progressed, plans and materials began to be firmed up, and a price began to be developed.

The other contractors they'd talked to had given them a price per square foot, without even coming to the house. "As we went on, the final price started getting locked in," Alex said. "When we were finished, the contractor said, 'This is the price, and you will not be paying any more.'"

He was a man of his word.

When, during the course of the renovation, asbestos was discovered in the ductwork, the contractor assumed the cost of removal, because, he said, he should have been aware of it from the outset of the job. When the municipality would not approve the plans for the kitchen eating area unless a beam or a column was installed to support the ceiling above it, the contractor gave Alex and Beth the choice and swallowed the additional cost.

A lot of contractors will demand that the contract be negotiated before they'll allow that work to proceed, but the ones who depend on referrals typically will not. Their contractor, who does 40 major jobs a year, does not advertise, but he did provide the couple with a list of 100 references and urged them to call. He also drove them to see a couple of houses he had recently completed where they could talk to the owners, and he provided them with a 12-page manual outlining procedures and even the basics of remodeling.

Beth acknowledges that the work always took longer than promised. For example, the kitchen, which was supposed to have been finished in 6 to 8 weeks, was completed in 11. So for four months, they lived on food from a toaster oven or used their neighbors' kitchens. To catch up after weather-related delays, the contractors' crews worked Saturdays. Sunday work is prohibited by municipal law. "If they were going to be late, they would call," Beth said. "If the inspectors didn't show and the workers couldn't proceed, they'd leave a note."

The contractor has a regular crew and always uses the same subcontractors, so he knows all the personalities and the problems that can arise and anticipates them.

No deposit was requested up front. Alex and Beth didn't begin paying until the work began, and then wrote a check each Friday for the work that had been completed that week as specified in the contract. They also would pay for the materials as they arrived, rather than pay the contractor, yet the price included the contractor's discount. The contract also specified a 100 percent, three-year warranty, but from what the couple heard from other customers, the contractor usually will come out after three years.

Then, there's the list of things that must be fixed before the job is completed according to the terms of the contract, also know as the punch list.

"Where most builders try to keep the punch list small, the contractor came out and made a list of 20 to 25 minuscule things that his crew spent two or three more days to fix," Alex said.

Alex and Beth remain enamored of the contractor and his crew, whom they would recommend to others and would use again. Their affection does have its limits, however. "The day the job was finished, I told them that I loved them, but I didn't want to see them anytime soon," Beth said.

14. IT'S ALL IN THE PLAN

Without one, your project is doomed from the start.

■ ■ ■

A colleague wanted a staircase rebuilt, so he hired an architect to draw up the plans. Because the contractor the architect used regularly would be busy for the next six months, the colleague tried to find another on his own. Only one contractor answered the call. After about ten minutes of amicable chatting, the colleague handed the architect's plans to the contractor.

"I don't use plans," the contractor said.

The colleague postponed the project six months, until the architect's contractor was available.

When you are dealing with a major renovation, such as an addition, you need to hire an architect to come up with a workable, sound plan that meets both the building code and your needs. Even when you are doing something less extensive such as bathroom remodel, you should pay a kitchen and bath designer $50 to $75 an hour for a few hours' work to come up with something that reflects both your wishes and the realities of what the remodeled room should accommodate.

If you need a set of bookcases, on the other hand, find a photograph of what you want, determine the dimensions, and hire a carpenter. Even a deck built by a contractor familiar with local codes may not need a licensed professional to design it—unless the client wants something special.

Contractors often have continuing working relationships with architectural firms. The larger contracting companies may even have an architect on staff. Such relationships may result in cost breaks for the customer. For example, when Alex and Beth Cerrato considered their two-story addition, they came up with ideas and were ready to contact an architect about coming up with plans. The contractor they were talking to about the job suggested using the architect with whom his firm regularly works. Hiring their own architect would have cost

$5,000 to $7,000. The contractor's architect did the plans for $3,000 and was available for consultation when problems arose or when changes needed to be made.

Projects might need to involve other professionals, such as structural engineers. We recently completed a remodeling project that involved adding a jetless Jacuzzi tub to the second-floor master bath, as well as a few minor changes. To hold the weight of the tub, 100 gallons of water, and a person, the floor underneath required additional support.

The first contractor we brought in didn't consider in his estimate how the tub would be supported, so we tossed it out. The second contractor went to the local lumberyard to look at what kind of support beams were available and which one would work the best with the least amount of reconstruction. He then called a structural engineer to look at what he was proposing. For $250, the engineer drew up an installation plan that was included in the municipal permit application.

Good contractors can think on their feet. The one we used also came up with an immediate solution to a drainage problem in the bathroom, involving the creation of false beams that allowed the drains to pitch at the correct angle to the soil stack. A good contractor can also play well with others, including architects, engineers, and subcontractors. A lot of consumers seriously believe that they can design complicated renovation projects with computer programs and save the cost of hiring a professional. These same people design staircases that don't quite reach the second floor.

These programs are most useful to consumers as an aid in getting their ideas across to professionals, but they were not designed and should not be used to replace trained architects. Just too much is involved in designing and building a house to relegate the process to a $45 program. No matter how user-friendly these computer programs are, their designs can't provide certain things.

One is creativity. Home design is much more than putting rooms next to each other. You need to have an understanding of how people use their space. In most cases, these programs only produce plain-vanilla, two-dimensional designs. It's also important to remember that a computer is only as creative as the person entering the data. When designing in three dimensions, an architect can create specialized, unique spaces that fit any homeowner's lifestyle.

Architects work with homeowners to take advantage of the home's surroundings. They have the expertise to determine how to incorporate the most magnificent views, to figure out what trees should be kept, and how best to use sunrise and sunset in the design. Architects also take climate into account. If the roof isn't designed to support a large amount of snow and you live in Buffalo, New York, you're in deep trouble.

Most homeowners are not familiar with the building codes in the area, and this can make designing a home dangerous and costly. If a homeowner makes changes later to meet codes, they can incur additional construction costs. In addition, a consumer who isn't familiar with construction is taking a huge risk, because the addition might either be dangerous to live in or financially impossible to build.

The bottom line: Your peace of mind is worth much more than the price of a professional's services. When you need one, hire one.

15. YOUR HOUSE, NOT THE POOR HOUSE

Never spend money if it won't boost your property values.

■ ■ ■

I'm part of that group of upwardly mobile baby boomers who are rich in earnings potential but poor in available cash. That means that banks are willing to lend me large sums of money. It also means that credit card companies are mailing me introductory offers for which I'm "preapproved."

Then, of course, there are those commercials on cable television filled with terrified people wanting help climbing the mountains of debt they have accumulated with the help of credit card companies and banks.

That, my friends, is known as capitalism.

Before Fannie Mae and Freddie Mac began supplying us with relatively low-cost mortgage money, people who wanted houses spent years saving enough money for a down payment. Some even scraped up the funds to be able to buy the house outright, without having to go to the bank president, hat in hand, for a loan.

But the availability of low-cost money has made us rather careless with the way we borrow and spend. A lot of us get into trouble, borrowing over our heads until we can only afford to make the minimum payments on our credit cards, if that.

What's the use of having a spacious master bedroom if you can't sleep at night, or a $60,000 top-of-the-line kitchen if everything you eat brings on indigestion because of your worries about debt?

Heavens' first rule: Never let a house own you.

The corollary is to be careful how you use the equity in your house. To make reasonable use of the value you have built up, use it to make reasoned and reasonable improvements to your house.

I'm a big believer in not tapping into the equity in your house for anything. Whenever I've refinanced out of a high-interest mortgage, I've shopped around until I found one with the lowest fixed interest rate and lowest origination costs and rolled those costs into the new mortgage. But the new mortgage has always been the prerefinancing balance plus $500 to $1,000 in origination costs. By lowering the mortgage payments, I've been able to increase savings or use the extra money to pay down or pay off credit cards.

If you can save for a project, delay the effort until you can readily afford it. This often isn't possible. Say you have a small house in a great neighborhood in a good school district with enough room for parents and one child, and then you discover twins are on the way. You have two options: you can buy a larger house or build an addition. You've determined after a search of the market that the addition is the least expensive and most efficient option, because what's available for sale would need lots of work anyway. That's when you get into debt. You have no choice, except to go there carefully enough to get out of it with the least amount of pain.

Remember: Never overimprove. Always make certain that what the house is worth after renovation will more than cover what it cost you to make these improvements, plus interest.

Let's look at some of the good ways and bad ways to finance your renovation project.

First, avoid using your credit cards. If you do use them, be reasonable and try to pay them off each month, rather than accumulating thousands in debt at 21 percent interest. You may use the cards for things needed for the project if you don't like carrying large amounts of cash or your checkbook, but pay them off monthly, or at least establish a manageable ceiling for credit card indebtedness. Make sure that, when credit card companies notify you that your limit has been increased, to immediately decline the increase in writing. Even if you never use the credit card to the maximum, the size of the limit can affect how much you will be able to borrow from less expensive sources.

This is truly easier than it sounds. Some consumers have no other choice than to use credit cards and pay until the end of time.

The second way to finance a renovation is with your savings. For the last 17 years, our savings have been devoted to paying school tuitions. Believe me, with college tuitions increasing every year, you'll need to sock away plenty starting when the pregnancy test turns positive if you ever expect to pay for a child's higher education. However, some people are able to save for just about everything. Usually, you can save enough for small projects, such as second-floor laundry rooms.

You might want to look into borrowing from long-term savings, such as a 401(k), especially if you are many years from retirement and your plan permits loans. My plan permits up to two loans up to half the total value of the 401(k). For example, if you have $100,000 in the 401(k), you can borrow $50,000. The interest rate is usually set at prime. In effect, you are borrowing from yourself, and the money can be cheap if the prime rate is low. In addition, if the stock market isn't doing well during the term of the loan, the interest you are paying back to yourself may actually be a better return. You can always increase the percentage of your paycheck that goes into the 401(k) to balance things out.

It's not the best option, of course, but it's a relatively easy and quick way to borrow money. You should always talk to your financial planner to see what he or she thinks before you act.

I'm not a great believer in debt, and I'm also in favor of doing things in manageable phases, such as renovating a kitchen over time to limit disruptions and keep strict control of money. I am that voice in the wilderness that no one ever heeds, however, so if you are going to borrow and renovate, do both wisely.

Additions, kitchens, family rooms, and the like are big-ticket items and require more funds than can be saved for quickly. For those projects, there are other options.

Sometimes, you may be able to increase the size of the mortgage to cover purchase of the house and the cost of a renovation project, if you can prove to the lender that the house will be worth at least the amount you borrowed after the work is completed. In one case, a relative obtained a $250,000 mortgage and a $50,000 construction loan. After the house went to settlement, the bank had the house immediately reappraised. The renovation hadn't even started, but based on the market and what the relative was planning to do, the appraisal set the new value of the house at $450,000. The loan officer himself came to the site a couple of times to "monitor" the progress. A separate account was set up for the renovation money. After each of the first two visits, the loan officer would deposit money into the account to pay for the work. By the third visit, the loan officer handed over all the money, because he considered my relative a good risk.

It was a little bank, since swallowed by larger ones. Bigger mortgage companies and the big banks wouldn't touch this kind of loan.

Fannie Mae, the nation's largest sources of mortgage money for lenders, has a variety of renovation loans and renovation and refinance loans that can combine what you need into a single first mortgage loan or a separate second mortgage. Details on those loans are available directly from the Fannie Mae Web site (http://www .fanniemae.com) or any lender who works with Fannie Mae.

Consider refinancing. By refinancing, you can cash out the equity in your house and obtain a mortgage, typically at a lower interest rate than you have and for little cost. Then you can pay for the renovations with the money you cash out. Make sure that the house that you'll have when the renovations are complete is worth more than the money you spent and your mortgage balance combined.

Also, home equity loans and home equity lines of credit are both available from just about any lender. You'll need to shop around for the best deals.

A home equity loan is a single lump sum, fixed-rate, fixed-term loan, usually at a higher interest rate than a mortgage. The home equity loan also is known as a second mortgage, because is secured by the house. If you can't make the payments, you can face foreclosure, just as with the first mortgage.

With a home equity line of credit, or HELOC, the lender decides how much you can borrow and for how long. Once you've set it up with your bank, you can dip into a predetermined amount of available cash whenever you need to, as easily as accessing your bank account. You can write checks or use your ATM card to withdraw cash or pay bills by debit. Meanwhile, you pay interest only on the portion of the credit line you are using, rather than on the full amount. Say the bank gives you a HELOC of $100,000, and you borrow $50,000 and pay back $25,000. That means you have $75,000 available. A HELOC typically has a variable interest rate. The HELOC is secured by the value of your house. You also can pay down your entire balance with no penalties.

For both types of loans, lenders cap the credit line at 80 percent of the appraised value minus the balance of the mortgage. In addition, the lenders look at your creditworthiness, just as they would with any loan.

If you are concerned about having your house held hostage, you can try an unsecured line of credit. The drawback is that the interest rate is higher than a home equity loan.

A couple of years after we bought our first house, we decided to do some work to make it more livable. We each took out a $5,000 personal loan from our credit union, at a fixed interest rate lower than the going rate for a 30-year fixed mortgage (then about 15 percent). The advantage was that we were dealing with a known entity and had savings accounts from which the principal and interest were deducted automatically each week.

Unfortunately, the job was a disaster and the end result was far from what we had been hoping for. Was the education we received worth $10,000 plus interest? We didn't think so then. But 20 years and two houses later, I think it was worth it.

16. POINT, CLICK, ANSWER

The Internet—and the dog, of course—are your best friends.

■ ■ ■

It was only a matter of time before the Internet got into the home repair and remodeling business in a major way. Not only can you find Web sites for contractors and Web sites about contractors, but you can locate hard-to-find materials online. You can even visit chat rooms to hash out those curious house problems for which there seems to be no cure.

Soon, someone may come up with a computer than can hold a hammer. Sound far-fetched? Not at all. Ever since Robbie the Robot made his film debut in *Forbidden Planet* in 1956, humans have held out hope for mechanical assistance with household chores. Robotics is making inroads in the automobile industry. Major builders are also using computers to design houses and to drive the assembly-line machinery that mass-produces the parts they design.

Until the day of the household robot, the computer's primary contribution to household maintenance will be information—who does it, how to do it, and where to buy it. That's where the Internet comes in. For contractors, the Internet may be a godsend, a relatively inexpensive and efficient way to run a business that will leave more time for construction and require less time to track down leads, deal with materials vendors, and manage finances.

The National Association of Home Builders believes that remodeling may outpace residential construction in annual volume of business by 2019. But it also emphasizes that historically, contracting businesses—except for the successful few—are not run on a sound business footing.

The remodeling industry is incredibly fragmented, studies show. Of the 880,000 businesses that can be considered involved in remodeling, 550,000 are single contractors with no payroll. About 40 percent of those 550,000 had gross receipts of less than $100,000. More than half the firms that are around at the start of any five-year period are likely to be out of business at the end. This means that the warranties you secured from contractor guaranteeing their work for a time after you sign a check might not be worth very much.

The Internet may offer a solution to helping contractors effectively manage their businesses. One Web site, Contractor.com (http://www.contractor.com), was launched in 1999. Contractor.com builds a Web site for a contractor free of charge. By providing a profile, the contractor will be listed in a professional database. The Web site will forward "referral-quality" sales leads for jobs that contractors want, and it has a directory of 800,000 contractors that can be used as a source for labor.

Contractor.com doesn't charge a fee for leads or sales resulting from leads. But contractors can pay a small monthly fee for higher placement in the directory. The site provides contractors with a personalized newsletter service for customers, e-mail, business software, forms and templates, marketing tools, and discount Internet service. It also offers Contractor University, through which contractors can enroll in Internet and teleconferenced classes covering estimating, production and scheduling, and sales and marketing.

Obviously, Contractor.com can be used by consumers, too. Especially useful is its list of contractors nationwide, divided into categories such as remodeling and "fun extras." The best thing about Contractor.com from a consumer's point of view is that it provides estimates for various jobs based on what the customer is willing to pay. For example, if you want to have a powder room built, the site provides three estimates based on how chic you want that powder room to be. Estimates can vary widely depending on where you live. Building costs are usually more expensive in New York City than they are in the Adirondacks, or in New Jersey than in New Mexico. So don't expect your contractor to come up with the price you saw on the Web site.

The number of consumer sites for locating "reliable" contractors is growing. One is ImproveNet (http://www.ImproveNet.com), a Web site based in Redwood, California. ImproveNet matches homeowners not only to prescreened contractors but to architects and designers as well. It, too, offers services to contractors on its ProSite, and it lets retailers and manufacturers use its site to market their products and services.

ImproveNet offers some cutting-edge consumer aids, such as a "lavatory laboratory," which allows homeowners to experiment with combinations of flooring, built-ins, and fixtures to create the bathroom designs to fit their budgets. Does it work? You may have better luck with it than I did. When I was looking for a contractor to add a tub to the master bath, the site was unable to give me a name of a suitable contractor closer than 50 miles from my house.

While Web sites such as Contractor.com, Handyman Online (http://www.handymanonline.com) in Beaverton, Oregon, and ImproveNet try to make contractor-consumer matches on a national scale, others take a regional approach, registering and vetting local contractors before listing them. The entrepreneurs who set up these sites are typically not contractors but consumers who had to deal with no-shows or contractors who never followed through on estimates, resulting in missed work, wasted time, and endless frustration. Some of these sites have a toll-free number for consumers.

ContractorNet.com (http://www.contractornet.com) started as local site in suburban Philadelphia several years ago as a telephone clearinghouse for local contractors, but grew into a major national site once it developed its Web site.

The Internet also is providing help for people interested in doing things themselves. RepairClinic.com (http://www.repairclinic.com) in Canton, Michigan, offers parts for major home appliances including washing machines, freezers, and water filters. The site has a RepairGuru—an experienced appliance repairman full of sage advice. Tips include placing a tablespoon of liquid bleach on the bottom of your dishwasher before leaving town for a week or more (so it won't smell) and warnings not to try mulching two-inch tree branches in your garbage disposal (one of his actual service calls).

There is also CornerHardware.com (http://www.cornerhardware .com) in San Francisco, designed to marry the services of the old-fashioned corner hardware store with the selection and convenience of the Internet. The site features live 24-hour and real-time e-mail chat support, how-to articles from home improvement experts, and easy-to-follow animations that lead the consumer through every step of the project.

Just about every major product manufacturer has a Web site, easily located by typing what you need into your search engine, seeing what comes up, and then refining that search with more information. Manufacturers' associations such as those who make windows, doors, roofing supplies, and tools also have informative and easily navigable sites.

Government Web sites provide information about building codes and permit processes, and federal agencies, such as the Department of Energy (http://www.doe.gov) are treasure troves of information on energy saving appliances. More are coming online every day.

Who needs Robbie the Robot when they have a computer?

17. NO JOB TOO SMALL

Not every job needs a contractor.

■ ■ ■

"No job is too small! Call 555-6724, 24 hours a day. . . ."

How many times have we seen ads in shopping guides and on bulletin boards in supermarkets for contractors making that claim? No job is too small, of course, until you talk to the contractor's answering machine and await the return call. It never comes, because, as one and then another and then another frustrated reader tells me, "They don't want to touch it unless it is a $20,000 bathroom remodeling job."

Let me tell you why contractors never call you back on small jobs. For the last several years, and long before the events of 9/11 convinced millions of Americans that their homes were safer places to be than just about anywhere, homeowners have been spending about $150 billion annually to get that kitchen of their dreams, put in that extra bathroom for the children, or finish the basement.

If all you have is a window that needs to be reglazed or a garbage disposal installed, what chance do you have?

You might think that even the overburdened remodeling contractors might be willing to return consumers' phone calls to guarantee that they will have work when they are not so busy. It's a tough idea to get across when times are good. Of course, we consumers aren't the brightest pennies sometimes, either. We wait to get our roofs repaired in the fall, when roofers are their busiest, or have our central air-conditioning system serviced right before the summer, just like everyone else, and then we wonder why we have to wait.

Why not consider the handyman (who can be of either sex) for small jobs that the contractors won't tackle? I don't mean that you should hire a handyman to service your heating and cooling system, of course, because the work could violate the warranty. Most handymen don't have the necessary technical training.

Handymen will rake leaves, paint one wall of a room, install a light switch, or build a bookcase. Some will install gutters or drywall, hook up a stereo, or load a dumpster. And they'll all hang pictures, so you won't need to call them later to fill the extra holes you've made in the living room wall.

The 1940s movie version had the handyman showing up at the kitchen door, hoping to make enough money to get by on, and then disappearing once he had. Times have changed. It's all business these days, with display ads in the local shopper, panel trucks with name and telephone number on the sides, signs in front yards, and answering machines.

As with contractors in good economic times, most handymen don't have a moment to spare. Why? Because there are lots of little jobs for which the typical homeowner has neither the time nor the expertise. Though the little jobs might seem big to the harried homeowner, to a contractor with a dozen or so employees and huge overhead, they aren't worth the trouble, but for rates ranging from $25 to $50 an hour, they are worth the handyman's time.

Some of the larger handyman companies, with a couple of employees, will take on two or three jobs a week, including building an addition with the help of the appropriate subcontractors. Most handymen want small jobs, however. They aren't licensed electricians or plumbers and typically don't handle work that requires a municipal permit. Handymen get most of their work by word of mouth, and most find that smaller jobs often lead to bigger ones. Sometimes, if they are good, people are reluctant to pass on their names for fear they'll get too busy. On the other hand, a bad name is easy to get, and a lot of fly-by-nights are out there, too.

People turn to handymen because they can't afford to pay the higher prices that bigger guys charge for small jobs. Case in point: I had a three-sided bay on my old house where 22 inches of crown molding had rotted out. Birds were nesting there in the spring. I called a roofer to repair it. When he finally arrived, the estimate was $1,600. I might have paid it. But another contractor was replacing a beam on my porch. He told me that the roofer was planning to hire a carpenter to do the job. The carpenter was charging $800. The roofer needed to make some money, so he was doubling the cost. I borrowed a ladder, went to the lumberyard and spent $20 for the piece of molding. It took me a couple of hours on a Saturday afternoon to install it.

Thus, in a sense, I became my own handyman.

Many homeowners do their own work until they get in trouble or run out of time. Unfortunately, many people call for help because they lack the confidence to do even simple, easy-to-do jobs themselves. What really surprised me early on is that some people even call for help assembling build-it-yourself furniture. They think they're saving money by buying a four-piece bookcase, then spending $25 an hour having someone else put it together. The less expensive answer is just to keep reading and reading the directions, then "dry fit" (assemble without tightening the screws) the pieces until you get a rhythm going and can finally assemble it yourself. If you get stuck in the middle of a job, it's unlikely that even a handyman will call you back, because they'll spend most of the first few hours on the job having to disassemble what you've put together just to find where you messed up.

Although they may not charge what contractors are asking, handymen aren't free. Depending on the job, they could charge you up to $75 an hour, plus travel time. Others charge by the job. Included in those charges is liability and vehicle insurance, Social Security, state and federal taxes, wear and tear on equipment and trucks, and expertise.

When dealing with handymen, the consumer needs adhere to the same rules that you follow with contractors. No matter how grateful you are to have someone arrive to tackle your project, if you don't like them, you won't be happy with the completed task, no matter how well it is done. Insist that the handyman provide you with a firm time when they will show up to start the job. You should insist that the handyman telephone you if he or she will be late. Although some handymen don't provide written estimates, you should ask for one. A written estimate is, in reality, the final price of the work to be completed unless you ask for changes in the job as it proceeds.

Because handymen tend not to specialize, make sure that the one you hire has done your job before. There's no point in financing a disaster. You also need to secure written proof from the handyman that he has liability insurance and workers' compensation and that you will not be liable if he is involved in an accident while on the job. You also should demand a reasonable guarantee of his work. Make sure that the handyman adapts his work schedule to yours, not the other way around. Insist that he take his equipment home at the end of the day, or reach an agreement where that equipment will be safely kept and out of your way. He needs to clean up after each day's work and at the end of the job to your satisfaction.

You've got to let him know that noise, especially sounds that are not directly related to the job, such as music or chat from a boom box, be kept to a minimum. If the handyman smokes, you may ask that all smoking happen outside, even if the weather is cold or it is storming, whether you smoke or not. The rule may sound unreasonable, but the handyman is working for you, and you establish the rules. In addition, workers who smoke on the job increase the risk of accident, such as igniting paint rags or your trash with a carelessly tossed butt.

Remember, you are paying the handyman to fix your house, not burn it down.

18. THAT'S NO LADY, THAT'S YOUR PAYCHECK

You don't have to take guff from anyone, especially the contractor.

■ ■ ■

Laura Philips Bennett, a former speechwriter for Jimmy Carter, owns a successful public relations firm with offices in Orlando and

Miami. Although she and her significant other, Michael, share their house, Laura owns it. When work is done on the house, she signs the checks.

That doesn't seem to matter to the people she hires to work for her, Laura says. "One contractor shows up at the house with a $50,000 invoice," she says. "'Here, little lady,' he says. 'Show this to your husband when he gets home to see if he agrees.' Now, I made the call, and I met with the contractor, and Michael isn't home, and still I have to get my husband's approval?"

When Michael is home but Laura is doing the talking, the contractors still look past her to Michael and ask him, "What does the little lady think?"

One of these encounters was with an air-conditioning contractor. "There was a guy replacing the kitchen window when the contractor arrived," Laura says. "The contractor had faxed the estimate for the air conditioner, which was going to cost $10,000, but seemed a little hesitant about coming to the house to talk to me about it. After he was there a while, he finally said, 'Little lady, I didn't want to come when you were here alone because I'm just wasting my time. I usually don't explain air-conditioning to women, because they just don't understand, so I have to explain again to their husbands.'"

At this point, the window installer was so engrossed in the exchange, he was stretched across the kitchen sink to hear the conversation better.

"So," Laura says, "you're going to accept a check with my name on it yet tell me I'm too stupid to understand what you're talking about."

"That's right," the air-conditioning installer replies.

"So how many customers do you think you lose with this kind of attitude?" Laura asks.

"About 10 percent," the contractor replies.

"And what are you doing about it?" Laura asks.

"Nothing, little lady. It's just business."

At this point, the window installer loses his footing and falls into the sink. When the contractor leaves, the installer gives Laura the name of another air-conditioning contractor, who ended up with the contract and Laura's check.

Now, besides wondering how tall Laura is because of all of the references to "little lady," you must be wondering how some businessmen can be so stupid.

First, Laura is 5′ 2″. Next, the problem doesn't seem to be with only men. Some businesswomen can be just as clueless. Laura points out that the architect/designer for the remodeling project, a woman, addresses Michael whenever she meets with the two of them.

Of course, not all contractors and builders are like the ones who seem to find their way to Laura's doorstep. Even so, a survey by the Fannie Mae Foundation, which was designed to determine whether women are more financially independent today than they were 25 years ago, found that supermarkets, medical providers, banks, colleges, and online services scored high for gender equality, but the mortgage industry and home repair and construction services failed the test.

The worst scores went to remodeling contractors and residential builders. Of those women surveyed, 57 percent failed them on fairness, and only 9 percent gave them an A.

Laura is not one to suffer fools gladly, and if you are a woman—whether married, single, or otherwise—you should not, either. The influence of women on the home improvement market is only bound to increase. By 2010, women-headed households are projected to increase to 31 million, or close to 28 percent of U.S. households, a study suggests. Furthermore, the number of single women homebuyers has doubled in the last 15 years, according to National Association of Realtors. In 2003, the last year for which data are available, 21 percent of home purchases were made by single women, up from 18 percent in 1997. Single women also accounted for 13 percent of all vacation/second-home buyers in 2003. One in five single women bought homes. The ratio for men was one in ten, the association reported.

More and more women are taking full responsibility for home improvement projects, whether doing the jobs themselves or hiring and managing professionals. Not all women are getting on the bandwagon, however. Among married women homeowners, 44 percent said their spouses were solely responsible for home maintenance, and 30 percent of all women homeowners said they were not very handy or handy at all.

A 2003 survey of more than 1,000 male and female homeowners, commissioned by Sears, found a "gap in confidence" between women and men in their ability to take care of a home problem. A majority of men (71 percent) said they were confident that they would know how to take care of a repair problem, while only 58 percent of the women surveyed said the same. That said, 71 percent of single female homeowners surveyed said that home maintenance was a major concern, compared with 33 percent of single males and 62 percent of married or cohabiting homeowners. More than half of women homeowners surveyed said it was important for them to learn more about home maintenance and repair.

Knowledge is power. Even if you never pick up a hammer, you should be familiar with which end you use and what you use it for. Or at least convince a contractor that you know something. If contractors are led to believe that you possess a wealth of information on how your project should be done, they're likely to treat you with respect—or at least look you in the eye.

Where is the knowledge that you need available? Start with the Internet. Real estate experts point out that minorities have made considerable use of the Internet to search for information on houses and mortgages because of the anonymity it affords. If you believe that you might be subjected to discrimination in a face-to-face meeting, why not choose a route that involves no commitment. Other resources that don't require direct contact include books and TV how-to shows. When you are ready to show your face, there are classes at home centers, and adult education programs.

What it boils down to is assertiveness. This is your project. It's your money, it's your house, and you'll have to live with whatever you get. You have to be in control of the process from the beginning to the end. To do this, you'll have to make absolutely certain that the contractor and the people who work for the contractor know who is in charge at all times.

It's you.

19. WORD OF MOUTH

There's an almost foolproof way to find a contractor.

■ ■ ■

Looking to hire a contractor?

Well, if anyone tells you to open the Yellow Pages, pick five names, and call them for estimates, then they are absolutely crazy. First, Yellow Pages are advertising. Advertising costs money—lots of it. How does an advertiser recoup that money? From customers, which means in the price a contractor charges you. And the bigger the company, the more advertising and the higher the costs. In addition, just about anyone can advertise—whether they are good or bad.

Am I suggesting that you not check the Yellow Pages or not pay attention to advertising? Not at all. I'm simply saying that it's not the most efficient way to find someone to do your work.

So what is?

I am an unapologetic advocate of the word-of-mouth school. This means that if you are looking for someone for a particular job, ask your neighbors, friends, or relatives for recommendations. If you are new in town, you might ask the real estate agent who sold you the house. Never ask the home inspector, who, if a member of a professional association, is not allowed to recommend anyone while working for you. No one who expects to remain an inspector will risk being so tainted, no matter how much they want to help. Don't be offended or get angry. It's just business.

Real estate agents are a wonderful source of information, because if they, too, thrive on word of mouth for new business and on providing good service to their clients for repeat business, they will work for you long after settlement day. They typically keep lists of various contractors and repair people that they provide to sellers to help get houses ready for the market.

Again, agents and brokers cannot steer you to contractors or repair people, because under the terms of the Real Estate Standards and Practices Act they can be subject to fines and also could lose their state licenses. That's one reason why listing agents provide sellers with a group of names on their list. The other is, as one agent told me, "If I give them just one name, they usually come back and complain about the person, and I have to give them another one."

But after the transaction is completed, they might be willing to share names of people they use. From my real estate agent, I obtained the plumber I used for 14 years and whom I recommended to friends and neighbors. My neighbor provided the name of an electrician. Another neighbor, a carpenter, built my deck. The decision was not based on proximity or because I didn't want to offend him by hiring someone else but on the quality of his work, both at his house and elsewhere. A true professional, even if living next door, would never be offended if you hired someone else. In fact, having a neighbor or friend work for you can be awkward, especially if problems arise.

Subcontractors who work on your renovation job are usually willing to do more for you. For example, the plumber I used on my bathroom remodeling job cleaned my clogged soil line to the sewer before the remodeling project began. He subsequently rescued me on a wintry Sunday afternoon after my old sump pump died, appearing, like the Lone Ranger, just as the water began rising through the cracks in the basement floor. In many cases, homeowners who are not completely happy with an overall job might be thrilled with the work of individual subcontractors. That can lead to bonds for life.

Word of mouth can be the best way to find people who do quality work. And before contractors with big advertising budgets burn me in effigy, let's look at what consumers are saying. In a 2003 survey commissioned by the Scott Paper Company and conducted by Opinion Research Corporation, 81 percent of more than 1,000 Americans questioned said they would be most likely to hire contractors based on recommendations from neighbors, friends, or relatives. No other referral source came close. In addition, most of the respondents actually checked references.

The survey, and the anecdotal evidence I've collected over the last 15 years, points to a love-hate relationship between consumers and contractors. Consumers need them but don't trust them. The survey identified the three top complaints about contractors: not showing up when they said they would, jobs taking longer than expected to complete, and waiting a long time for work to be scheduled. Even homeowners Alex and Beth Cerrato, who have very little bad to say about the contractor who handled their six-month addition, acknowledged that "the work always took longer than they said."

But love and hate work both ways.

I was speaking to an association of contractors a few years back. Unfortunately, by the time I spoke, three hours of open bar and a really bad comic had preceded me. The contractors were not in the mood to hear what consumers were thinking. This meant, of course, that they were willing to be frank about what bugged them.

Estimates.

Studies of the remodeling industry by the Centers for Housing at Harvard show that the vast majority of the nation's nearly one million independent contractors are small fry, with maybe one person who does most of the remodeling work themselves with the aid of subcontractors. Workdays are long and filled with unpredictable events. Plumbers get tied up on other jobs and can't come till the next day, delaying the contractor. Materials don't arrive on time. The building inspector cancels an appointment, and the job grinds to a halt.

These factors limit the number of jobs the typical contractor can do in a year. When consumers complain that contractors are only interested in bigger jobs, this is the primary reason. If you want someone to handle a smaller job that doesn't need a permit or a licensed professional, I'd suggest a handyman.

The bottom line: The contractor has little time to waste estimating jobs that they know they'll never get. The only time available for doing estimates is after the day's work is done or on the weekends. That's also when the contractor typically returns phone calls. The contractor makes appointments when convenient for the customer. They must discern what you want, because few consumers seem to be able to explain themselves clearly at the start. Then they have to find time to take all the information you've provided, do research, find the materials, come up with alternatives, plot out your job, and estimate costs. Throughout the process, the contractor knows that you have four or five other contractors doing the same thing, and you will likely go for the lowest bid.

Can you, as a consumer, even begin to understand the effect this has on the contractor?

I'm not saying that getting a couple of estimates on a job is wrong, especially when the project is a large and complicated one. I'm just saying that "calling five contractors out of the telephone book and asking for estimates" is not the best use of your time.

This is why I advocate word of mouth. You first talk to people you know who have had similar work done. You ask them to provide complete information on what the job entailed—from products, to labor, to time spent, to how the contract was written—including how well they and the contractor and his subcontractors got along and any problems that arose during the job and how they were solved.

Make sure you know the good and bad, and promise that all you are told will be held in the strictest confidence. Armed with that information, you make the telephone call to the contractor or contractors that have been recommended. You tell the contractor up front who recommended them, you describe what you want done clearly and concisely, and you say when you want the work done.

Be flexible on the time frame. If you really want this person, you have to cut the contractor some slack. You also need to be completely honest. If you are talking to other contractors, you need to say so. Your final decision should be based on more than saving a few dollars.

When you hold your first meeting, find out something about the contractor's background and recent jobs, and share your previous experiences with remodeling projects—the good and the bad. A working relationship based on detailed knowledge of the participants involved will go a long way to get the two sides over any rough patches as the work proceeds.

Does word of mouth work 100 percent of the time? Absolutely not. I once needed someone to repair a faulty outlet near my first-floor bathroom. (I am terrified of electricity, although I have done some minor work over the years.) I asked a group of neighbors. One recommended an electrician in the neighborhood that she had used and was planning to use again. I called the electrician several times, but he didn't return any of the calls. Finally, the chief electrician at my job, who lived nearby, stopped on his way home from work and replaced the outlet in ten minutes.

A few days later, I walked past the house of the neighbor who had recommended the electrician. A different electrician's van was parked in her driveway. The one she had recommended had failed to return her calls, too.

20. KEEP IT LEGAL

You need permits, and that's the contractor's job.

■ ■ ■

Maybe if I tell you a scary story about people who didn't bother getting necessary permits for a renovation project, you'll be inclined to do the right thing.

A few years back, I wrote an article about decks, one on a city rooftop and the other in a suburban backyard. Having had experience obtaining permits for my own deck, I assumed that the city homeowner hadn't obtained a permit while the suburban homeowner had. Two weeks later, I received a telephone call from the building official in the suburban town. The deck had no permit, and the official had just delivered a cease-and-desist order to the subject of my story.

One edge of the deck was less than ten feet from the property line and needed a zoning variance to be legal. It didn't get one. The home-owner had to raze the $10,000 deck and start the process again—under the eyes of the building official. The deck was rebuilt, but it wasn't easy and cost more than double what it should have.

I once lived in a city in which the department responsible for issuing and overseeing permits had a reputation for being, shall we say, less than angelic. Much of the private residential construction was done without going through the permit process, which typically involved spending two or three days in city hall, being passed from bureaucrat to bureaucrat until someone looked at your plans and stamped them.

The problems didn't end there. Each phase of any major renova-tion project had to be inspected and approved by the building official before the next phase started. If the building official failed to show, completion of your project could be delayed by days or weeks, and you and your contractor would have to renegotiate your agreement if the delays begin to cost the contractor money.

Lots of illegally built porches, decks, bathrooms, and additions began springing up, and some of these projects were not built to code—something a building inspector would have spotted had a per-mit been issued. Decks collapsed in rainstorms. Improperly con-nected gas lines led to explosions. Deadly fires were sparked from poor electrical work.

But, instead of getting to the root of the problem, the head of the building department stationed inspectors outside home centers and lumberyards to follow cars and trucks filled with building materials back to their owners' homes. There, if the homeowners did not have the proper permits, they would be fined and the materials confiscated.

The effort was short-lived, thanks to vocal complaints by retail-ers and higher-level city officials, because most detainees were sim-ply replacing broken toilets or building bookshelves, not work that required permits. Instead, the next commissioner scheduled an am-nesty period in which people who had built illegally could apply for permits after the fact without penalty. However, problems persist.

Suburban contractors won't work in the city, and the ones who agree to work there often require the homeowners to obtain the permits themselves.

Melissa Rooney and Vic Gatmaitan faced this problem when they wanted to build a deck. They obtained a good estimate, but the contractor wouldn't deal with their city's building department. So Melissa took a long lunch hour and went to the department's office, prepared to settle in for a long wait. A department engineer walked over as she was starting to take her seat, voluntarily drew the plans to Melissa and Vic's specifications, based on the deck builder's plans, and then rushed through approval of the permit.

Melissa was several months' pregnant. Sometimes you just go with the flow, no matter how unfair it seems to everyone else. The finished deck was spectacular, replacing a porch in desperate need of demolition. It greatly enhanced the value of their house.

I know I've already told you not to renovate to sell, but remember this, too: when you sell your house, your municipality usually checks its records to certify that the house has no code violations. An inspection is often involved. Anything illegal will delay or even prevent a sale until things are made right.

Here are two more things to remember when you renovate. The first is to hire a contractor who is well known to the local building department and who has developed a solid working relationship with officials. This means that contractor knows all the rules, all the staff— including the assistant answering the telephone—and can run through the permit process and the inspections quickly and easily.

The second is to make absolutely certain that the contractor handles the entire permit process from the start to the final inspections that result in the certificate of occupancy that is required before the municipality signs off on your project. Don't take the contractor's word for any of this. Go to the building department yourself before you even begin looking for contractors. Find out whether your project is feasible under municipal code and what the process involves step by step.

When you do find a contractor, call the building official and run the contractor's name by them. Try to discern from what the official says how they truly feel about the contractor, even if the official says nothing good or bad. The tone of the official's voice, or the length of the pause after you mention the contractor's name, can speak volumes. Have you ever changed dentists? The first hour of your first appointment is typically a litany of what the previous dentist did wrong. Building officials follow the same route when talking about contractors.

The upside to keeping it legal is that you won't have to spend a lot of money to raze what you've built or on lawyers in a drawn-out court case that you probably won't win. The downside is that the municipality will be aware of everything you do and will likely raise your assessment and your property taxes.

And remember, if you get an inspector on a bad day, nothing your contractor does will make the official happy.

Permits ensure that your contractor does the work properly. Although requirements vary from place to place, permits are typically needed for structural changes to your house or its mechanical systems—installation of central air-conditioning, for example. Permits also establish standards. They tell you how your project should comply with building codes, what kinds of materials are acceptable, the proper way things should be installed, and structural requirements.

Remember, local codes rule. While these codes are typically based on current national and international codes, they may not follow them to letter. For example, the code in one town might say that only basements with eight-foot ceilings can be finished as bedrooms, while the next town may require nine feet and the next one seven. All three towns, however, will likely follow the same rules governing emergency exits from the basement bedroom. Any variation should be part of your contractor's repertoire.

You are likely to need more than one permit. A central air-conditioning system will likely require separate plumbing and electrical permits as well as a general building permit for the ductwork. A general building permit typically covers the sizes of rooms, the location and size of doors and windows, the amount of light and ventilation, and how it is achieved, and fire protection, including rating of insulation, wall materials, and whether or not the smoke alarms have to be hardwired.

Permit fees are based on the cost of the project and are paid either by you directly or by the contractor and included in the price. Those fees are paid after the plans and the cost estimates for your project have been submitted and approved. When the fees are paid, the contractor and the building official will set up tentative inspection dates, then firm them up by telephone once the work begins and the contractor has a better idea when the work will be completed.

Usually, 48 to 72 hours notice is required, because the inspectors are handling other work. Make sure that the contractor keeps all inspection appointments. It matters little if the inspector is late or doesn't show up, but if the contractor makes the same error, the inspector will not be happy and that could affect your project.

Things can't go on forever, so the building department typically grants permits for a certain period—usually six months. If there is a delay and more time is needed, a written request for an extension is the norm, and you and your contractor had better have a pretty airtight reason for it, such as weather delays or problems with delivery of critical materials.

Other requirements vary. You'll need to find out how many sets of plans to provide; if the permits are issued all at once or in phases as the work is completed, inspected, and approved; and even in what window the official notice of construction should be posted.

When the work is completed to the building department's satisfaction, you will be granted a certificate of occupancy. You need to make sure that one is issued and that the contractor is at the house to make sure that one is issued. I once employed a really fine contractor who completely forgot about the certificate of occupancy. A year after the work was completed, I received a notice from the municipality that I might be fined if I used the tub in the master bath without one.

The permit process sounds like a pain, but it is necessary. The majority of building officials I've dealt with over the years behaved like professionals, but I've heard some nightmarish stories about others.

A colleague was helping her elderly parents build a new house behind their old one on property her father had owned for 50 years. Before the inspector would sign off on the project so that the parents could take their possessions out of storage and move in, he wanted some trees he said were in the wrong place replanted. It was a matter better handled by Mother Nature. The saplings to which he was referring were not planted by the family but were seeded by other trees. It didn't matter to the official. The couple and their daughter replanted the saplings, and the certificate of occupancy was granted.

21. A HANDSHAKE IS NEVER ENOUGH

Never do anything without a written contract.

■ ■ ■

I'm not a lawyer, nor do I play one on TV. Therefore, I would be violating state law somewhere if I offered you legal advice.

I can, however, relate a couple of stories from experience emphasizing the importance of a written contract. I can also tell you that experts who suggest that you might be able to get away with just an oral agreement if the value of the work is less than, say, $1,500 must have a lot of money to throw away. For most of us, with mortgages, bills, childcare costs, and the like, $1,500 is a lot of money.

I don't care what is being done and who is doing it: get it in writing. And if you are concerned enough about the agreement you are about to make, hire a lawyer to draw up a contract between you and your remodeling contractor, or have an attorney review the agreement, either before you sign or at least before the rescission period expires so you can pull out without losing anything.

Here is another of those scary stories I use to make my points.

Many years ago, I needed a new roof on my house. I went through the traditional method of finding a roofing contractor—the Yellow

Pages, three names, three estimates. The contractor I chose seemed to know what he was talking about. When I proposed a written agreement, he became indignant, however, saying that his reputation and the references he provided (three of my neighbors) were better than a written agreement.

I stupidly agreed to forgo the written agreement.

At the start, everything worked out as promised, except that the contractor was not part of the crew, nor did he show up until the end to check out the work. He climbed a ladder, looked around, and said the work was fine. He then provided me with a document that guaranteed his job for ten years.

During the next heavy rain, I looked out the front door and saw water pouring off the edge of the roof into the neighbor's mailbox. I called the roofer's answering machine for several weeks and wrote him letters. No response. The problem continued, and the neighbor became angrier.

I called a second roofer, who climbed his ladder and began pointing out flaws in the other roofer's work. The most important, and the one causing my problem, was that the opening in the downspout that handled the runoff from two other roofs and mine had been tarred over.

I left that message for the first roofer. Two of his workers showed up the next day, but instead of opening up the downspout, they began installing flashing at the corner of the roof to prevent the water from pouring into the mailbox. Their solution would have allowed the water to pond in the middle of the roof. Water finds its low point, which, in this case, would have been our third-floor front room.

The long and the short of it: We had no written contract, so in small claims court, it was the roofer's word against mine. He even argued successfully that, by installing the flashing "dam," he was adhering to the ten-year guarantee. The repairs made by the second roofer cost $1,000. But there was a written contract for that job, I assure you.

Written contracts offer both you and your contractor the best protection from misunderstandings that might lead to an unfinished, poorly done job and prolonged legal battles. Before you sign the contract, if you don't want to have it reviewed by a lawyer, look over it yourself and change or delete sections that cause you concern, especially ones that might cost you money unnecessarily. Then sit down with the contractor and negotiate these sections. Because you haven't signed the contract, you have plenty of time to iron out these difficulties.

Even after the contract is signed, you have a three-day cooling off period. This is called a *right of rescission* and is guaranteed to consumers under the federal Truth in Lending Act. The right of rescission gives you three business days after signing the agreement to cancel it, if the contract was signed anywhere except the contractor's place of business. Your right of rescission is enforceable in court.

If you are about to spend $150,000 for an addition, make sure you spend a little more and have a lawyer either prepare the contract or at least review the one provided by the contractor. $150,000 is too large a sum to risk to just a handshake, no matter how firm it is.

22. WHAT'S YOUR NAME AGAIN?

Don't spare any details in your written contract.

■ ■ ■

I suppose it sounds kind of dumb, but very early on in the contract, you will have to list your name, address, and telephone number and the contractor's name, address, and telephone number.

It's not such a dumb idea.

I once hired a contractor at the urging of a friend of mine. The contractor was the friend's brother. The friend, who had been in a number of businesses over the years, including remodeling, promised that he would act as an unpaid overseer to make sure the work was done properly.

I met the contractor at the brother's place of business. When introducing him, my friend called the brother by a different last name than his. Being too polite for my own good, I didn't inquire further, assuming that perhaps they were half-brothers with the same mother but different fathers.

When it came time to sign the contract, which the contractor didn't seem all that eager to provide or sign, I noticed that the address and telephone number were for my friend's business. When I asked why, my friend replied, rather sheepishly, that it would be easier getting in touch with his brother through him. (These were the days before cell phones.)

The bottom line: The reason my friend and his brother had two different last names was that his brother, a veteran contractor, kept changing his name to avoid disgruntled customers, unpaid subcontractors, and angry suppliers. He had no place of business, other than his house, which was OK, but had an unlisted home phone number to throw off his creditors. Because of his checkered past, few subcontractors would work with him, and few suppliers would extend him credit for materials. He had to ask contractually for half of the estimated cost of the project at the signing, which I refused to give him. His previous problems had led him to work with subcontractors who were glad to have the work, all of whom asked to be paid separately for their work when it was completed. The suppliers wanted the materials paid for before delivery.

The job did not go well, although from what I've told you, a bad experience was what you'd expect. He said the job would take ten days. Three months later, I was still trying to get him to come back to finish a radiator cover and tile work on the kitchen counter. My friend had no idea how to get in touch with him, so my friend finished the work for him.

Not so dumb, is it? Get that name and number down in that contract, in case you need to know where to send the papers for the lawsuit. It's important that your name, address, and phone number be included as well. In addition, make sure you know what kind of business it is—a sole proprietorship, a partnership, or a corporation. In

the last two cases, you'll need to make certain that the person signing the contract represents the partners or the corporation, so that all
the provisions of the contract will be honored.

Be sure that the contract states specifically that the remodeling
contractor is independent and not your employee. Otherwise, you
might responsible if a subcontractor or an employee of the contractor is injured on the job. The contractor should provide their Social
Security number for financial reasons. The price of the work specified in the contract should include sales tax, if applicable, and all
other incidental charges, including the cost of permits.

Another thing that should be established up front is the starting
and completion dates. As I've pointed out elsewhere in this book, the
best contractors are often booked well in advance, so you'll need to
assume that your job will begin once the others are well in hand. But
once the job starts, you need to get a reasonably firm date in writing
about when it will end. The work will not begin until the rescission
date passes, but that is usually only three business days after the contract is signed. If a couple of weeks go by and nothing happens, then
you can expect future delays as well.

Things happen, to put it politely. Contractors, like television me-
teorologists, cannot predict the weather, and if you are digging a
foundation for the addition and every day features a torrential down-
pour, that foundation will be delayed until the weather is dry and the
concrete can be poured without washing away. What you want to
prevent is the contractor getting started on the next job before he finishes yours.

Some experts recommend bonuses for work finished early or on
time, and penalties if the contractor blows the deadline. Few contractors, unless they are working for the government, will agree to
such clauses. They know what can happen, and they need to get
across to you what is real and what is fantasy when it comes to completion dates.

To reduce disruption and keep the job moving, you may want to
set tentative completion dates for certain phases of the job. For example, the foundation will be dug by one date, the foundation will

be poured two days later, and framing will begin the following Saturday. That way, you can look at the contractual completion dates and reality and see how long you'll be heating up pizza in the microwave.

Another way to keep the job moving smoothly is not to start changing your mind about how you want the addition built or what you want for countertops just as the contractor prepares to install the granite.

Remember: The contractor's promise is only as good as the reliability of their subcontractors and suppliers. An overbooked plumber might not be able to meet whatever deadline the contractor has established, and, frankly, the contractor won't be able to a thing about it but plead on the phone to the plumber and apologize to you.

As long as the contractor has your phone number and you have the contractor's.

23. NO DEPOSIT?
THE CONTRACTOR WILL RETURN

A good contractor doesn't need a hefty deposit to get started.

■ ■ ■

A colleague recently asked me if I'd heard the story of the unscrupulous contractor who asked for and received a deposit of $45,000 to build an addition for a desperate young couple expecting a baby.

"They never saw the contractor again," I said.

How did I know? When a contractor asks for a hefty deposit, then no matter what the job is, something is wrong. Although the contractor might not be an outright crook, they might need your money to pay for products and subcontractors for another job in progress, especially if the contractor underestimated labor and materials costs and the contract with that other customer is firm. A lot of contractors are wonderful craftspeople without much business sense, and they are forever getting into trouble on jobs because of it.

The contractor my colleague talked about will serve time in prison, but, unfortunately, the young couple, like the many others the contractor bilked, will not be getting their money back. The contractor has no attachable assets, and no amount of suing will squeeze blood out of a stone.

A reliable, solvent contractor will not ask for a big deposit. In fact, the smart ones will not ask for a deposit at all but contractually arrange a pay-down schedule—either once a week for the work completed by the end of that week or at points in the project when a prearranged phase is completed. The size of those payments should be arranged in advance.

The smaller the project, the less likely you'll be asked for a deposit. Now, if you've special-ordered a one-of-a-kind fixture that the supplier would never be able to unload on anyone else, and you've arranged with the contractor to pay for materials, the contractor might ask for the money up front. Be suspicious of demands for big deposits, and don't pay them, even if it means that the contractor walks. I know it is pain in the neck to start the process over again with someone new, but if you let the contractor dictate to you, you are just asking for trouble.

The price of the job specified in the contract should only change if the customer asks for changes and the contractor agrees to those changes in writing. Any changes, no matter how minor, should be reflected in the contract, and both sides should sign off on them.

Let's talk just a bit more about money. I've already provided some options for financing your remodeling project. Let me suggest that, if the contractor offers to help you find someone to provide financing for the project, decline politely and firmly. It's not that I'm accusing these contractors of anything. All I am saying that for the sake of clarity and to avoid any misunderstandings, the person who does the work and the person who finances the project should not be connected in any way.

If being able to proceed with project hinges on obtaining financing, there should be a clause in the contract that states that the agreement is not binding unless you are able to secure funds on terms you consider acceptable.

One more point: You should obtain a list of the suppliers and subcontractors the contractor will be using, including their addresses and telephone numbers, so you will know who these people are and how to get in touch with them in case of problems. You also should obtain, in writing, what the contractor will do to protect you from liens in case the suppliers and subcontractors aren't paid. The best way to protect yourself against liens is to hold back the final payment until the contractor supplies written proof that all the subs have been paid for the work they did on your job. This is where release-of-lien forms, signed by all the subs and suppliers, would be appropriate. Some experts also suggest making the last payment to the contractor as large as possible—10 percent or more—to guarantee that the contractor will pay the subs in order to be paid themselves.

Speaking of clarity and avoiding misunderstandings, every contract needs to clearly spell out what is known as the *scope of the work* to be performed. For example, if the project involves remodeling a bathroom, the contract should include as many sentences as necessary covering every detail of the project so nothing will be left to interpretation.

As noted in Chapter 20, the contract also should state that it is the contractor's job to obtain all permits and necessary inspections, as well as the certificate of occupancy that the building code officials will provide when all the work is completed to their satisfaction. The contractor also should provide written proof, attached to the contract, that he and his subcontractors have valid construction licenses, workers compensation coverage, and the general liability insurance or bonding required to work in your municipality.

The contractor should also state in writing that he or his company exempts you from liability for any injury suffered on the job by employees, subcontractors, and even the people delivering materials. You'll need to state contractually who is responsible for damage to your property or your neighbors' property. You'll also need to specify the hours and days when work will be permitted, to limit the amount of noise you and your neighbors will have to put up with.

The contract has to establish where workers and delivery trucks can park. It also must state who will be responsible if materials are stolen and where those materials and contractor's tools should be stored for safekeeping.

Daily cleanup must be provided for in the contract. "Broom clean" is never enough. As much of the day's debris must be removed as can reasonably be expected. If you have toddlers, you don't want wiring exposed or nails and screws lying all over the floor. Spell out what you mean by *clean,* and make sure everyone who works in your house is aware of the rules.

The contractor also must specify how, where, and how often he or she will dispose of demolition materials and other waste generated during the job, including removal and disposal of hazardous wastes, known or unknown. Remember, some municipalities hold the homeowner liable for illegal disposal of hazardous wastes, and ignorance is no defense. That's why it is better to have all of this down on paper, rather than buried in your backyard under the cover of night.

Finally, if there is a problem, make sure that you and your contractor discuss it immediately and try to resolve it amicably. Sometimes, problems cannot be resolved. Therefore, the contract must include specific provisions for *alternative dispute resolution*—either arbitration or mediation. This means that you and the contractor agree to bring in an acceptable third party to try to resolve the dispute without going to court. If that doesn't work, make sure that you have kept specific dates and times and a accurate record of the conversation about the problem, as well as a letter sent to the contractor spelling out your complaints and suggestions for a resolution, and the contractor's response, if any.

Your goal is have the contractor perform the work as agreed or to have the contractor pay to have the work completed to your satisfaction by someone else. If you need to go to court, make sure that the judgment includes legal fees and court costs.

I know it's a heck of a way to do business, but sometimes it's the only way.

---

24. DON'T TAKE NO FOR AN ANSWER

If you want something, there's usually a way to get it.

■ ■ ■

At the start of our first renovation almost 25 years ago, I asked the contractor for plaster walls and ceilings in the second-floor bathroom he would be renovating.

"No one does that anymore," he told me, "and it's real expensive anyway. Use drywall."

I then asked for six panel interior doors for each of the upstairs rooms.

"No can do," he replied. "They don't make them anymore."

Because I was young and gullible, and I just wanted these people out of my house, I didn't put up a fuss. I was wrong. Had I pressed the contractor, or had I done some legwork myself, I would have found out he was lying on both counts.

If you look carefully, there are plenty of plasterers. The plasterers' union continues to train and produce new ones. Many older plasterers work well past retirement age. Many starving artists also support themselves as plasterers.

And the doors?

Of course, they still make them, as a visit to a lumberyard or home center would have shown me. If you are willing to do a little work to get them looking good, you can buy them cheaply at a salvage yard.

Contractors tend to shun what they don't know, and this is often the case with new products. A colleague asked me what she should ask her roofing contractor to do to reduce the heat in her attic in the summer. I recommended a new material, TechShield® radiant-barrier sheathing, a Louisiana Pacific (http://www.lpcorp.com) product that, according to the manufacturer, keeps attic spaces cooler by deflecting 97 percent of the sun's heat. The result is a 20 percent savings in air-conditioning costs. A few days later, she reported that the contractor had never heard of it and didn't think it would work. He'd decided not to use it, without so much as even looking at Louisiana Pacific's Web site or literature available at the home center.

Contractors say no for three reasons. The first is that they don't want to be bothered. The second is that they don't know the answer but have what seems to be a good reason not to spend time tracking it down, because it might mean a delay in getting your job done and moving on to the next one. The third is that they are so set in their ways that any attempt by a customer to get them to reconsider their ideas is regarded as an insult.

Don't waste your money on inflexibility. I'm not denying that customers can be pains in the neck and often want things that are truly impossible to supply. I simply mean that contractors should be flexible and willing to go the extra mile to offer real explanations of why things can or cannot be done. If the contractor had said, for example, that it would be better to replace the plaster with a more moisture-resistant product such as cement board or green board, I would have accepted it. By dismissing my request out of hand and insisting on drywall, which wicks up water like a sponge, the contractor was being the kind of jerk about which consumers constantly complain.

In my next house, I had a deteriorating 15-by-10 plaster ceiling in the living room replaced by another plaster ceiling. The total cost was $800, and the project was completed in just a few days with minor disruption. Sure there were differences in materials used—the contractor didn't use straw and horsehair as binders—but it was plaster.

The attitude of my longtime plumber, Marcel Paillard, is more what you should be looking for in any contractor. We wanted to replace a very ugly bathroom vanity with a pedestal sink that was more in keeping with the age of the house. We supplied the sink. As he was removing the vanity, Paillard remarked, "Most people are replacing pedestal sinks with vanities, but I'll do everything to make this thing work." He did, relying on the reflection of the back of the pipe in a mirror to help him make a connection.

A good contractor never says no. A good contractor is resourceful. A good contractor can look at problem and come up with a solution. You, the homeowner and employer, should be able to give the contractor a hand in helping to do a job that meets with your satisfaction and is also one in which the contractor can be proud.

For example, if the contractor says that they've never heard of what you are asking for, show them a photograph, download appropriate information from a Web site, provide telephone numbers of others who will provide technical data and relate their experience with the product or material.

You may be the one who is able to find the particular craftsperson the contractor may need to complete the job to your specifications. Even if you find a craftsman, things may be more complicated than you ever imagined. For example, failing plaster is often caused by problems with the material underneath. For a few feet down a hallway, the plaster is on top of brick, and then the material underneath shifts to wood lath. Masonry expands and contracts differently than wood, and as each shifts, cracks appear in the plaster.

Plaster was pushed between the pieces of wood lath for added strength, and to help the topcoats adhere better. That plaster, too, deteriorates over time, especially when moisture finds its way into walls and ceilings. Nails holding the lath to the framing loosen over time, and the weight of the plaster on the weakened lath causes sagging.

To get the new plaster to the original appearance, everything underneath has to be made right. And that takes time and costs money, more than if the plaster was replaced by drywall.

You see, renovations should strive to preserve the architectural integrity of the house. If you have a Queen Anne–style house with a slate roof, you should try to replace or repair the roof with the same kind of slate or with new material that looks like slate unless you are up on the roof eyeballing each shingle. Although some of the original manufacturers of old-fashioned shingles and tile are still in business, they produce only a couple of popular styles. Special orders are prohibitively expensive. For example, some trim pieces on a tile roof cost up to $60 each.

Enterprising contractors turn to salvage, often tracking down salvagers around the country to find what they need. They also borrow pieces from parts of roofs that aren't easily visible, without compromising the integrity of the roof.

In fact, borrowing from places that aren't easily visible solves other problems. If your contractor is trying to match original molding or flooring and just needs a few inches or a couple of feet, they can take it from a closet. If an entire room's worth is needed, however, the contractor will take the molding profile to a salvage yard to find a match. If that approach comes up empty, the contractor can take that same profile to specialty lumber yard and have it made. For specialty moldings, it can take a few days to a couple of weeks to obtain a profile cutter from a machine shop, so the contractor should get the ball rolling long before the material is needed so the missing material doesn't hold up the job.

The cost of the molding is based on the price of material, the cost of the cutter, and the set-up time. The more molding you order, the more cost-effective it is. It can be expensive, but if you are willing to pay for it, you should get anything you want.

That is, of course, if what you want is within reason.

25. MATERIALS MATTER

Get the pieces of your project in order before you start.

■ ■ ■

Anything you want should mean just that. It shouldn't mean anything that the supplier has in stock, no matter how much it costs.

This means that when writing the contract, the name, manufacturer, model number, and price of each product must be specified. If you want a fiberglass entry door made by a specific manufacturer costing $800, you have to put it in writing. That should even include the door hardware.

If the contractor's supplier doesn't have what you want, then you and the contractor need to reach a mutually agreeable arrangement about how and from what source that fixture or appliance will be coming, and who will pay. The ideal situation is for you to pay for the product or material on delivery but for the price still to include the contractor's discount. It may not be possible to obtain a discount if you are not dealing with one of the contractor's regular suppliers, but if the alternative supplier wants to do further business with the contractor, there may be some willingness to cut you a break.

Consumers are bound to shop for products, and one convenient place to go looking for items for your renovation is one of the major home centers. If you find a particular product that you want and propose that you buy it at the home center, you might be lectured by your contractor on "home center quality."

Many contractors and repair people say that the products that a manufacturer supplies to home centers tend to be of lower or, if not lower, then different, quality than the products the same manufacturer provides to wholesale suppliers, even if they are the same model. I once asked a representative of a plumbing fixture manufacturer whether or not this was true, and the response was, "There is no simple answer," which means yes and no.

My advice is to go directly to the manufacturer's Web site or request a product catalog with detailed information, so you can have the complete picture about anything in which you are interested. Provide a copy of that information to your contractor. Then go to the home center to see whether or not what is being sold matches the specifications of what you are looking for. Have the contractor present that information to the supplier. If both have the same product, but the home center price is lower and there is no difference in the manufacturer's warranty, then buy from the home center.

It may be that the products may be exactly alike at both places, but the one at the home center doesn't have exactly what the contractor needs for installation, while the one from the supplier is the total package. That's what you need to know before you make your informed decision.

When the contractor orders materials from suppliers, the quantity he requests typically includes extra for waste and breakage—usually 5 to 10 percent more than the job requires. Let me urge you to ask the contractor to order enough so that if something happens down the road and a section of material has to be replaced, you have enough to match and replace it.

Here's another scary story from the Heavens's saga.

I bought tile for a bathroom floor in 1990. In 2001, just after the agreement was signed to sell the house, a leak developed somewhere in the drain line between the bathtub and the soil stack. To find it, several square feet of tile had to be removed. When I went to replace the tile, I found that the tile store had gone out of business and that the manufacturer had stopped making the tile.

Long story short: I ended up buying slightly larger tile and cutting it to size. I finished grouting the floor 12 hours before settlement. During the presettlement walk-through, the buyers said it looked "funky." The leak, by the way, turned out not to be in the drain line but in the supply line to the toilet. The work was unnecessary and added to the stress of selling and moving.

Buying extra for future repairs goes for everything, including trim.

When it comes to paint, be aware that each batch of it tends to differ slightly from the previous or next batch. Therefore, you may have to repaint an entire wall rather than touch up a damaged spot. It is still wise to keep a record of all the paint used in your project.

Make sure you order products well in advance of the installation date, if you want to make sure your project begins and ends on time. For example, kitchen cabinets typically take eight to ten weeks from the time you order them to arrive. Custom windows usually take four to six weeks to arrive after you've chosen them.

Always make sure that what you've ordered is in stock. If the item is on back order, try to get the supplier to commit to a delivery date. Once each product arrives, make certain that the contractor checks that the product is new and in good shape and that all the pieces necessary to be installed properly have arrived. A missing widget can delay installation and hold up an entire project.

Let's talk about warranties. The contract should mention two different kinds of warranties.

One is a warranty on workmanship. This means the workmanship of the contractor, their employees, and subcontractors. States, and sometimes even municipalities, specify a minimum warranty period of, let's just say, three years. Call your local building department and ask what the law mandates, just so you can make sure that what the contractor is specifying in the contract is not less than what's legally required. The better contractors usually offer a longer warranty than the law requires.

The other kind of warranty is the manufacturer's, which is typically extended only to the original consumer owner. It may apply to all mechanical parts of a product under normal use for as long as the original purchaser owns the house, or it may be a one-year warranty on parts and labor. The manufacturer's warranty may be voided if the item was installed improperly, was intentionally damaged during installation, or is repaired by unqualified repair people. For example, a manufacturer's warranty on a heating system may require the purchaser to use only the company's repair people and parts, and it may be voided if the equipment is not regularly serviced.

Whatever the requirements are, they should be specified in the contract. That goes for the big-ticket items especially, but make sure the contract is as detailed as possible to ensure there are no misunderstandings.

Remember: It is what *you* want. You are the one signing the checks.

26. NOTHING LASTS FOREVER

Expect things to break. Even new things.

■ ■ ■

After living with a woefully inadequate kitchen for ten years, we borrowed enough money from my 401(k) for a new one. With the help of an electrician, a plumber, and a designer provided by the cabinet supplier, I was able to transform an ugly, virtually useless room into something we weren't embarrassed to own. Included was a dishwasher, which is something we had done without for more than a decade. I had the dishpan hands to prove it.

Three years passed, and circumstances led us to sell the house and move. A month after the agreement of sale had been signed, I removed the wooden kick plate to vacuum under the dishwasher. The back of the kick plate, and the floor behind it, were wet. Because the dishwasher had only a one-year warranty and I hadn't opted for extended maintenance, it cost $250—more than half the cost of the original dishwasher—to repair.

Imagine a world where things lasted forever!

In the 1951 British film, *The Man in the White Suit,* Alec Guinness portrayed a mild-mannered inventor who came up with a fiber that never wore out. That meant, of course, that clothing would last forever—or until it went out of fashion. The result would be that most manufacturers and retailers would shut down. The indestructible fiber never made it past the laboratory door. Clothing, like just about everything else we own or use, wears out eventually and requires replacement.

So it is with the myriad pieces of all sizes that make up the giant jigsaw puzzle we call a house. According to the National Association of Home Builders, "A well-built home can last for centuries, but many of its parts must be replaced or refurbished on a regular basis."

With this thought in mind as well as the adage, "They don't make things like they used to," I can assure you that building products and appliances are improving every day, thanks to technological advances and better quality control. And, as products improve, they become so inexpensive—my DVD player in the workshop cost me just $30—that you can throw a broken one away and buy a new one for much less than one of those extended warranties.

Many problems with modern building products—or just about anything—typically arise only when the products are installed incorrectly or maintained badly. You need to follow directions or insist that the installer follow them.

Manufacturers determine the life of a product by testing or by customer surveys. Sometimes they do both, along the lines of *Consumer Reports*. Most data on appliance longevity is gathered by trade associations. The associations compile manufacturers' surveys completed by customers when they buy appliances, asking how long the customer owned the previous washer, dryer, or dishwasher. From the responses, they determine high, low, and average life expectancies. Because of all the variables involved in use, the averages aren't always on the money, but they are pretty close.

Warranties aren't based on average life expectancies, however, so if the April 1996 issue of *Appliance Statistical Review* (http://www .appliancemagazine.org) says that your dishwasher should last ten years and it dies after nine, don't expect to get a new one for free. Warranties for appliances are typically one year and cover all parts and labor, and that's it. Some exceptions—for example, the sealed system tubing in a refrigerator that carries the coolant—are covered for longer. Manufacturers assume that people will neither use a product as they would expect them to nor read instructions.

Paint, too, undergoes extensive testing. The Rohm & Haas Paint Quality Institute (http://www.paintquality.org) in Spring House, Pennsylvania, for example, conducts outdoor tests on paint all over the world as well as testing it under laboratory conditions. Paint is tested for color and gloss retention and resistance to dirt and mildew. It is applied to all kinds of wood surfaces, vinyl, and aluminum to determine durability. After extensive testing, it has been determined that exterior paint on wood, brick, and aluminum surfaces will probably last seven to ten years.

There are caveats, though, and they will be discussed in a subsequent chapter on painting. For instance, there needs to be sound surface preparation before painting. In paint jobs on older homes, you see a lot of paint failure because moisture is getting behind the paint, so you have to take care of that.

It all boils down to variables. Concrete is formed and poured on site, so there are a lot more variables contributing to its life expectancy. By reducing the number of variables, concrete producers have learned that the life expectancy of their products will increase. They accomplish this by establishing training programs and developing specifications for mixing and applying the material.

For instance, the Portland Cement Association (http://www.portcement.org) has developed a blue-ribbon warranty program for driveways—certainly one element of the home that undergoes more wear and tear than a lot of others. If a contractor has completed the training program and follows product specs to the letter, the driveway is guaranteed from defects for the first five years.

Some concrete products last longer than others. Concrete roof tiles these days typically have lifetime guarantees from manufacturers. The new concrete wall systems being developed might have similar guarantees, once all the variables that would affect such a pledge are determined.

Exposure to the elements, frequency of use, and maintenance typically determine life expectancy. According to the National Wood Window and Door Association (http://www.nwwda.org), an exterior door typically will last 25 to 50 years. If that door is protected by some sort of overhang—like a pent eave—the life expectancy jumps to 80 to 100 years. If, however, the door is exposed to degradation from rain, snow, expansion, contraction, and decay, then life is shortened to 25 to 30 years.

Smaller items tend to last longer than big-ticket ones. If a $400 faucet comes with a lifetime guarantee, there's a very good chance that it really will last that long. On the other hand, cars rarely seem to last much past the last payment.

27. HOMEOWNERS, SWEET HOMEOWNERS

If your home increases in value, so should your insurance coverage.

■ ■ ■

So you've spent thousands of dollars turning your house into the one you've longed for. Before you relax and begin enjoying what all that money has bought, you'll first need to think about whether your investment is adequately protected.

Meaning, of course, that you have to question whether your present homeowners insurance policy meets the needs of your renovated house. More than likely, the coverage is out of date. It was based on the purchase price before renovations. Even then, it may not have been adequate. Studies have shown that few homeowners completely understand what their insurance does and does not cover, nor do they have enough of it. If disaster struck, what the insurance company would pay to rebuild would not include the thousands of dollars you've spent to create the house you want.

The solution is to have the insurance company write a new policy based on reality. That will likely involve a visit by an appraiser who works for the insurer. The appraiser's job is to determine the replacement value of the house based on its current condition, then pass that information back to the company.

Companies that provide homeowners insurance periodically review customers' policies to determine whether adjustments should be made. While consumers sometimes complain that these changes are designed to increase revenue or to make up for losses from disasters such as hurricanes and tornadoes, insurers say that coverage adjustments can improve response time, get the right amount of money to the customer quickly, and reduce the number of lawsuits over insurance claims.

After you've completed a major renovation may be a good time to consider shopping around for competitive rates, says the Insurance Information Institute (http://www.iii.org) of New York, which represents the country's major insurers. If you've kept your coverage with a company for several years, you may receive a special discount for being a long-term policyholder. Some insurers will reduce premiums by 5 percent if you stay with them for three to five years, and by 10 percent if you remain for six years or more. Shopping around is one way to reduce rates. Others include raising your deductible and buying home and auto insurance from the same company to get a discount.

The institute cautions that, too often, coverage is based on market value—the price for which a house might sell. Factors that affect market value are location and the quality of the school district, but neither has much to do with the cost of replacement value. In addition, the replacement value is determined differently for older houses and newer ones.

Recent construction consists of materials that are readily available, and this means that insurance tends to cost less than that on existing houses. Older houses, however, have features and materials that are not easily replicated. For instance, one of the original features of a house might be a newel post at the bottom of the second-floor staircase that is an example of one-of-a-kind craftsmanship. To replace the post, coverage would even have to pay for making the hand tools used to make it. But the client would be given the option of having an exact replica or a more modern replacement made. The same is true with replacing plaster walls with drywall. To find costs of older materials, appraisers visit sites like salvage yards.

The insurance company's appraiser has many other concerns: age and condition of the roof, age of the heating system, the condition of the electrical and gas service, coverage and quality of the security system, and the number and location of smoke alarms. If the heating system is a combination of steam radiators and gas forced-air and is also relatively new, then the risk of fire is minimal, and there is a very low chance that the system will break down during the winter, resulting in damage from frozen and burst pipes.

The insurer looks favorably on houses with security systems, especially those constantly monitored by alarm companies. Such systems can reduce insurance rates annually by 15 percent to 20 percent, according to the Insurance Information Institute.

Insurers handle reviews of insurance coverage in different ways. Some leave it up to the homeowners to notify them of changes, or they send standard forms to be filled out and returned for the companies' review. A growing number are now doing on-site appraisals, using these "loss evaluations" to determine actual replacement value as well as make recommendations to the homeowners about security or fire protection.

In addition to having enough insurance coverage for your renovated house, you also should be concerned about whether or not the contents are covered. Say you have a piano. It might not be a one-of-a-kind instrument or an antique, but you need to ask if your policy would replace it if it were destroyed. Most policies do not have limits on replacement coverage for musical instruments. Contents are often insured for 50 percent of the total value of the house, with a $10,000 limit of jewelry and the same limit on silver.

Most insurance companies require separate appraisals for items of jewelry, art objects, and antiques when those items reach a certain value threshold—$50,000 or $100,000, for example. That appraisal is not provided by the insurance company. Typically, these appraisers are accredited by one of three nonprofit organizations: the American Society of Appraisers (http://www.appraisers.org), the Appraisers Association of America (http://www.appraisersassoc.org), and the International Society of Appraisers (http://www.isa-appraisers.org). Appraisers usually charge by the hour. By law, no appraiser may charge a percentage fee based on the value of the objects appraised.

When hiring an appraiser, referrals should be obtained. For insurance purposes, an appraiser should evaluate each item based on replacement value, not fair market value. Your insurance agent should receive a copy of the appraisal report. Even if you don't need an appraisal, insurers recommend that a complete record of your house's contents be kept. Periodic inventories should include sales receipts or estimates of the current cost of a comparable item. Photos or videos of the contents and their location should be included. The list and photos should be kept off the premises—in a safe-deposit box at the bank.

Standard coverage is for loss by theft or fire. If you misplace it, it's your loss unless you have a policy that covers such losses. Insurance companies don't want to pay claims if they don't have to, so they try to help homeowners look for ways to avoid damages, according to the Insurance Information Institute. These ways include seasonal maintenance, including developing a routine to check systems and clean gutters. Swimming pools should be covered when not in use to reduce the chance of accidents.

When windstorms approach, take all loose objects indoors. When on vacation, even if the house has a security system, have a friend or the police check it periodically. Vigilance also is important when a house is being renovated. Fire extinguishers should be available to prevent small fires from getting bigger. Don't disconnect the burglar alarm or fire alarm while work is underway. Try to keep unauthorized visitors away from the site, even curious friends or neighbors. The contractor should be aware that no one should be on site without your express permission. Make it plain that if anything is missing or damaged, it is the contractor's obligation to make up for the loss.

If that doesn't do the trick, nothing else will.

■ THINGS TO REMEMBER

26. Hire an architect for major renovations. For smaller projects, a designer will do.

27. If you hire the contractor first, see if the contractor has a working relationship with an architect. It may reduce costs.

28. Use computer design programs for ideas only. They cannot replace professional expertise.

29. Architects know whether it can be built or not. They also know building codes and environmental issues and concerns that determine how it can be built.

30. Never let a house own you.

31. Never use credit cards to finance a home renovation.

32. Be sure that what the house is worth after renovation will more than cover what you spent, plus interest.

33. Use the Internet as a major source of information about everything.

34. Having trouble finding a contractor for your small project? Consider a handyman.

35. When hiring a handyman, follow the same rules you would when employing a large contractor.

36. Don't let contractors bully you. Learn as much as possible about what the project will entail before the first meeting. Never be afraid to bluff about the extent of your knowledge.

37. Stay in control of the renovation process from beginning to end.

38. Referrals from friends, coworkers, and neighbors will get you a contractor.

39. Don't hire a neighbor because they are a neighbor. Hire a neighbor because they are the best choice.

40. Check those references.

41. Don't get more estimates than necessary. Contractors don't have time to waste on jobs they know they'll never get.

42. Be flexible on the time frame. No job ever runs on schedule.

43. From the first meeting, make sure that you and the contractor develop an unbreakable line of communication.

44. Never renovate without the necessary permits. It will cost you more than double if you have to demolish and then rebuild.

45. Make sure your contractor is responsible for all permits and inspections.

46. Never work without a written contract, even for little jobs.

47. Hire a lawyer to draw up a contract or review the standard one if you have any concerns.

48. A contractor's promises are only as good as the reliability of their subcontractors and suppliers.

49. A reliable, solvent contractor will never ask for a huge deposit in advance.

50. Pay for materials on delivery, but make sure the price includes the contractor's discount.

51. Unless your contractor can prove beyond doubt that what you want doesn't exist, insist on it until it is delivered.

52. Renovations should strive to preserve the architectural integrity of your house.

53. Make sure that all materials are ordered well in advance of the start of construction so they will be delivered on time and not delay the project or inspections.

54. Make sure the renovations are included on your homeowners policy.

PART 3

STOP, LOOK, AND LISTEN

. . .

You may be asking yourself why Mr. Know It All is lumping environmental issues and systems problems together in the same section of this book.

It's a fair question, and it has an easy answer: Whether the problem is mold, termites, faulty wiring, bad roofing, or broken plumbing, it needs to be taken care of or, at the very least considered, before you start renovating.

It stands to reason, doesn't it, that if you are planning to add a $60,000 kitchen, you have to make sure that there's no mold behind the walls caused by a slow roof leak that has ruined the insulation and encouraged the termites happily chewing through your floor joists to move up the food chain? And that's just the start.

Allan Hasbrouck, whose adventures in homeownership are touched on in Chapter 5, recalls that he and his wife were discussing cosmetic changes to the house one day when the clouds opened up to a rainstorm of Biblical proportions. He went to the second floor of his three-story house and watched water pour down the walls from their rotted roof. The cosmetics were put on hold until the roof was replaced, at great cost.

We can be forgiven for having this aversion to establishing priorities based on the realities of the situation. We're only human, and we like to dream. We want a house we can turn into this century's version of Versailles, and then we are shocked when find that we own the Bastille and that we are under siege on every side. Whenever you consider a renovation project, the rule is: assume the worst, and then hope for the best. Most of all, stay calm. The vast majority of problems with a house can be dealt with, even though someone will always try to convince us otherwise.

The biggest concern among homeowners these days has to be mold, or at least that's what my readers seem to talk about a lot. Some people are so frightened of mold that when they see a few black dots on a basement wall, they think they have to burn their houses and possessions, just like the people they've seen on the TV news. It doesn't occur to them that a brush dipped in bleach and water, a properly sized basement dehumidifier that keeps the humidity below 60 percent, and a little regular maintenance are likely to keep those little black dots from spreading or even reappearing.

Mold is the issue of the day, leaving older environmental concerns on the back burner. I asked a real estate agent how concerned today's buyers are with lead-based paint, asbestos, and radon. His answer: It depends on how much people want the house. In the sellers' market of the last five or six years, when little inventory is for sale and multiple people bid on every home available, buyers put environmental concerns aside to get the edge on the competition. In fact, some people will spend 15 minutes in a house and then put down a $10,000 deposit contingent on absolutely nothing—not roof, not electrical, not termites, not mold, whether or not the furnace works—just so they can shut out other buyers. It is a very dangerous and potentially expensive way to do business.

What are you buying? You can't begin to know until you've lived in a house for a while, even if a home inspector and other experts go over it carefully before settlement day. As I've pointed out already, new homes are not problem-free, but older houses tend to have more problems, especially if they've been neglected. How do you know the extent of those problems? You can't always trust the sellers, who are, after all, trying to get the best price for their house, to be completely up front when they fill out those state-mandated real estate disclosure forms.

To be honest, the sellers themselves may not be aware of the problems. If you live in a house for a long time, you tend to get so used to problems that you forget about them. Buyers usually end up having to fix these problems first. Problems need to be fixed before you start spending huge amounts of money on improvements.

Forewarned is forearmed. So roll up those sleeves, expose your forearms, and get fixing.

28. DANGER, WILL ROBINSON!

Before you renovate, you need to eliminate the bad stuff.

■ ■ ■

Over the years, humans have come up with lots of what appeared to be good ideas that ended up being very bad ones. One of the most obvious was using lead as an additive in paint so that it would adhere to surfaces better. Another was using asbestos as insulation around heating pipes. Then there are the problems created by nature that we've only recently discovered. I'm talking about radon.

We will tackle two other problems of modern homeownership—toxic mold and indoor air quality—in Chapters 30 and 31. Right now, I want to address the Big Three. I suggest that, well before you begin any renovation project, you tackle lead paint, asbestos, and radon first.

Let's stop a minute. Real estate agents tell me that homebuyers in a booming sellers market seem less concerned about these three issues and are more than willing to forgo all but the notifications of rights to inspect required by federal or state law. Even when radon is a concern, a buyer will negotiate with the seller for a certain sum to remedy the problem after settlement, then hold on to the money and never get the work done.

The health problems involved, of course, directly affect you and your family. But there is another consideration, one very important to the success of your renovation process. If a contractor comes across asbestos in the course of the job, and the asbestos may be disturbed because of the work, the job will stop until the material is removed safely. Obviously, additional expense will be incurred by the homeowner, because most states require that asbestos be removed by a contractor certified to perform the work.

Asbestos is a problem only if fibers are released into the air. An experienced contractor will be well aware of the danger and can probably recommend safe ways to test whether your old ducts are insulated with asbestos or if the condition of the asbestos warrants removal. There are safe ways for a homeowner to take a sample of a suspected area and send it off to a lab. If you take an asbestos sample, make sure the surface is completely wet by using water mixed with a few drops of liquid detergent, and then carefully scrape two or three small samples into a plastic bag with a zipper lock.

The same is true for testing lead-based paint. There are home tests available for radon as well. The best course is to contact your municipal health department for names of labs and to find out what local, state, and federal agencies regulate testing and removal.

Depending how extensive the problem is, you may want to move out of the house while the problem is being remedied. The work area is always contained in some way, usually with plastic sheeting so no fibers escape into the air, where they can linger for a long time. The asbestos contractor handles cleanup and disposal in a sanitary landfill that is designated for hazardous wastes, typically supervised by your state's environmental protection agency.

Similar precautions and disposal methods are required for lead-based paint. It has been 25 years since the federal government told paint manufacturers to reduce the lead content of paint to a trace .06 percent. But more than 75 percent of all homes in the United States—about 42 million built before 1978—contain a greater amount of lead contaminants. Not until 14 years after the ban did the government finally recognize that contaminated dust from lead-based paint was the primary cause of lead poisoning in children. The Residential Lead-Based Paint Reduction Act, which became law in 1992, established standards and programs to rid housing of lead-based contaminants. The result is that 26 million fewer homes have lead-based paint since the legislation was enacted, according to the federal Department of Housing and Urban Development (http://www.hud.gov).

The reason to rid your house of lead-based paint is a simple: the health of children, especially those under six years of age. A high level of lead exposure—more than 69 micrograms per deciliter—can result in convulsion, coma, and death. Even low-level exposure affects the central nervous system, especially in developmental stages, and can alter intelligence, motor control, hearing, and emotional development. Parents should consult a doctor for advice. A simple blood test can detect high levels of lead, and testing is important for children at ages one and two as well as for older children and other family members who have been exposed.

How does one test for high lead levels in the house? One can begin by looking for obvious signs. Peeling, chipping, chalking, or cracking lead-based paint is a hazard and needs immediate attention. Lead-based paint may also be a hazard when found on surfaces that children can chew or that get a lot of wear and tear, such as windows and windowsills, doors and door frames, stairs, railings and banisters, and porches and fences.

Lead-based paint in good condition is usually not a hazard. But lead dust is often invisible to the naked eye, and it can form when lead-based paint is dry-scraped, dry-sanded, or heated. Dust also forms when painted surfaces bump or rub together, such as on opening and closing windows or doors. Lead chips and dust can get on surfaces and objects that people touch. Settled lead dust can reenter the air when people vacuum, sweep, or walk through it.

Home testing kits are available for about $10. One home test kit uses sodium sulfide solution. You place a drop of the solution on a paint chip. If lead is present, the chip slowly turns darker. However, no official agency suggests that you rely exclusively on those tests. A more reliable test uses an X-ray fluorescence (XRF) machine to determine whether paint contains lead. Still, this test is not always reliable either. It can cost $500 or more, depending on the size of the house and the number of readings needed (often 300 or more). Laboratory testing tends to be the most reliable. It can cost $20 to $50 per sample.

HUD says that action to reduce exposure should be taken when the lead in paint is greater than 0.5 percent by lab testing or greater than 1.0 milligrams per square centimeter as determined by an XRF machine. Removal of lead-based paint requires a contractor certified by the state, and the process is similar to that for asbestos.

Radon is in a category by itself. The best that can be said about radon is that it is a colorless, odorless gas. The worst that can be said is that, according to some medical experts, radon is responsible for almost 10 percent of all lung-cancer cases reported in the United States annually. Somewhere in the middle stands the homeowner. And, according to real estate agents, lawyers, and radon experts, the homeowner isn't sure what to think.

According to the Environmental Protection Agency (http://www .epa.gov), radon is present in elevated levels—higher than the federal limit of 4 picocuries per liter of air—in nearly 1 of every 15 homes in the country. This radioactive gas, created from the natural decomposition of uranium in soil, rock, and water, moves up through the ground and into a house through cracks and holes in the foundation. Then the gas remains trapped in the house.

Many health experts consider federal standards excessive. In most European countries and Canada, radon is not considered dangerous until it exceeds levels of 10 or even 20 picocuries per liter of air. This discrepancy has been enough to create a controversy over the effects of household radon on health.

The EPA recommends that all houses being bought or sold be tested for radon. Congress in 1988 passed the Indoor Radon Abatement Act, stating that, "It is the goal of the United States that all homes, schools, and federal buildings be tested for radon."

Tests fall into two categories, according to the EPA. Long-term tests last anywhere from 91 days to a year. A long-term test will give you a reading that is more likely to tell you your home's year-round average radon level than a short-term test. The quickest way to test is with short-term devices. They are kept in place from two to 90 days, depending on the device. And, depending on the device, the test may require that all windows and doors stay shut. Though not as accurate as the long-term test, the short-term ones should be used to determine whether further testing is needed.

Radon levels in a home can be readily lowered for $500 to $2,500. In most cases, systems with pipes and fans are installed that don't require major changes in the home. Most new homes already come with such systems. Such systems prevent radon gas from entering below the concrete floor and the foundation. Similar systems can be installed in homes with crawl spaces.

Both professional testers and remediation contractors must be certified by the EPA. If radon concerns you and your home shows evidence of high levels of the gas, it might be worth your while to have a radon remediation system installed if the walls are going to be opened anyway. Even if the problem doesn't bother you now, it could be a problem when you sell your house down the road.

29. UP ON THE ROOF

Without a solid roof, everything underneath is wasted.

■ ■ ■

A well-built and well-maintained roof is critical to the health of every structure—be it house, church, shopping center, or corporate headquarters. Builders, designers, and manufacturers are constantly working to develop problem-free roof systems. The improvements come in many forms, including new design-load standards and innovations in roofing materials and ventilation/insulation techniques. Knowing what's available can save you money.

Most new roofs are designed to meet or exceed the load standards for a particular geographic area. The standards address what happens when the snow falls straight down or when it blows and drifts, for instance.

Roof-system designs vary nationwide. No roofer in the Northeast would construct a house without gutters and downspouts. In relatively rain-free Southern California and Arizona, however, few houses have them. In the West, tile is a popular roofing material; in the Middle Atlantic and Midwest, fiberglass-reinforced asphalt is king; and in New England, roofs are usually made of wood shakes.

The trend is to make existing roofing materials better. Roofing materials of metal, clay, and fiberglass won't chip or peel and are light, strong, durable, and fire-resistant. Fiber-reinforced cement, for example, is a noncombustible roofing material that is also lightweight.

In the old days, the fiber in a shingle was asbestos. It was a source of pollution as shingles deteriorated, but they did last 50 to 75 years. Now, shingles made of eucalyptus cellulose fibers impregnated with silica and Portland cement mimic slate at about two-thirds the cost. While fiber-cement shingles have about the same 50-year life expectancy as Pennsylvania gray slate shingles, Vermont slate lasts 100 to 150 years. But fiber-cement is about 30 to 50 percent lighter than slate and easier to install.

Framing has changed. Wooden roof-truss assemblies nowadays are produced in factories that are often hundreds of miles from building sites. The advantage of mass production is that standardized parts are of uniform quality, they cost less than on-site assembly, they use less wood, there is less wasted material, and they are quicker to install.

Amid growing concerns about exhausting lumber supplies, many builders have turned to steel in roof construction. Besides steel's cost and availability, the steel industry maintains that steel roofs offer the advantage of being more durable in areas vulnerable to earthquakes and hurricanes.

New products facilitate roof ventilation. For example, one new product is used to insulate and ventilate asphalt-shingle roofs installed on underlayment nailed to plywood or oriented strand board. In typical roof construction, decking is nailed to the truss assembly and the underlayment to the decking, with the shingles on top. What the underlayment, typically roof felt, does is to prevent rain or melting snow from leaking through the roof deck into the interior of the house. In this system, the new product, a glass-reinforced foam board with a flat bottom and channels on top that let air pass through, is an innovation.

This kind of venting ventilates and insulates an area between the roof decking and the plywood sheathing to prevent moisture buildup.

Asphalt shingles have a 20-year life under normal conditions; proper ventilation ensures it.

Underlayment prevents moisture from entering a building. This barrier also prevents water vapor from a variety of sources from exiting outdoors through the decking. In the winter, moisture is carried upward by warm air. When it comes into contact with the attic side of the ice-cold sheathing, it condenses. The warm air passes through the decking, but the moisture remains on the underside of the decking and accumulates. This action creates two problems that combine to drain your bank account. The wood used in the roof trusses and sheathing is like a sponge, sopping up and retaining every bit of moisture it comes into contact with. The trapped moisture will rot and warp the decking and leaks will develop.

Outside, on the roof surface, something else is happening, especially during the winter. The warm air that is escaping through the roof decking from the attic melts the snow on the roof, which trickles down to the frozen gutter and refreezes. This process continues until a dam of ice is built up that exerts pressure at the edge of the roof and the lower tier of shingles. As this ice expands and backs up closer to the warm part of the roof, it melts once more and finds its way through the underlayment and decking by way of leaks created by moisture buildup inside.

The solution to this problem is proper ventilation, proper insulation, and some added insurance—a product known generically as ice-and-water shield, a self-sealing bituthene waterproofing membrane with a strong adhesive underside.

As much as 70 percent of home heat can be lost through lack of insulation. The kind of insulation—batts and blankets, rigid-board or loose-fill—and the amount is determined by the anticipated heat loss or gain, cost, and code requirements. In addition, a vapor barrier should be installed on the side of the insulation that remains warm in winter, especially if the outdoor temperatures average 40 degrees Fahrenheit or below in the coldest winter months and the relative humidity within the house is a constant 50 percent.

The trick with insulation is not to overinsulate, and that should be controlled by ventilation. The standard developed by the Federal Housing Administration (http://www.fha.gov) is that attics with a ceiling vapor barrier must be ventilated with at least one square foot of vent area for each 300 square feet of ceiling. (Netting used to prevent pests from entering attic space is included in the equation.)

There are three kinds of vents—soffit, gable, and ridge. To help the process, some homes have turbine ventilators operated by moving air and attic or whole-house fans, which operate on electricity and are triggered by thermostats. For added protection, ice-and-water shield can be installed at leak-prone areas of roofs. According to roofers, this water shield, which is another form of underlayment, is installed about two feet up from the edge of the roof. However, W.R. Grace (http://www.grace.com), the first company to manufacture the shield, suggests that certain leak-prone areas, such as the hip or a low-slope roof, require an application deeper than two feet. In addition, Grace recommends that the shield be installed on both sides of a valley, along rake edges, around skylights and chimney bases, and on the ridges.

30. A MOLDY OLDIE

Don't let that stuff on the walls scare you.

■ ■ ■

Our search for tighter, more energy-efficient houses has backfired on us in a couple of serious ways.

One is poorer indoor air quality, to which increases in respiratory problems and allergies have been attributed. The other is mold. Mold is only one factor that compromises indoor air quality, but because the effects of mold often need to be cleaned up on a large scale, it requires its own chapter.

When houses were leaky, air moved through the walls, and wet wood dried quickly and completely. Although wood loses strength when it gets wet, the strength is recovered when it dries. Before insulation, the ability of houses to dry out was greater than their propensity to get wet. Now that homes are tight and they get just as wet as they always have, the potential to dry completely and quickly is much less, and moisture can accumulate behind the walls.

Moisture is the key ingredient for the presence of mold. Water incursion can be caused by floods, leaking roofs, or pipe leaks, but mold growth can be caused as well by the sustained presence of moisture from condensation or periods of relative humidity above 60 percent.

Mold is quickly becoming one of the biggest sources of both litigation and liability in the real estate industry. One by-product has been the growing unwillingness of insurance companies to write new policies, and their willingness to exclude coverage of mold from existing policies.

This doesn't mean that we have to do without insulation and shiver. Houses can be made energy-efficient, but ventilation must be installed to control indoor humidity levels and the growth of mold. We also have to make sure that houses don't get as wet.

It is not as easy as it sounds, however.

The chief exterior sources of water are snow, rain, and improper drainage. One inch of rain falling on a 2,000-square-foot footprint equals 1,247 gallons of water. If your area receives an average of 40 inches a year, just 1 percent of that finding its way into the interior represents a lot of water. There are many indoor sources of moisture as well, including cooking, breathing, and houseplants. Remember, the problem has to do with water, not the quality of construction materials, even though some materials can accelerate mold growth.

Not every mold is a potential hazard. Still, some people, such as asthmatics, are more sensitive to certain kinds of mold, especially when it is airborne. Can it hurt you? Yes, under the right conditions. Is it a new problem? No. As experts will tell you, mold is even mentioned in the Bible. Without it, cheese wouldn't age, and Alexander Fleming would have never discovered penicillin.

The chief concern of late has been with black mold. While less common than other molds, this one is more dangerous to humans because, given the proper environmental conditions, it can create multiple toxic chemicals called mycotoxins. These toxic by-products exist in the spores of the mold as well as in the tiny fragments that can become airborne. People may inhale and ingest these toxic spores. Fortunately, according to the Centers for Disease Control and Prevention (http://www.cdc.gov), few case reports show that toxic molds inside homes can cause unique or rare health conditions such as pulmonary hemorrhage or memory loss. A causal link between the presence of a toxic mold and these conditions has not been proven, the agency says.

Mold can become a problem overnight. Research shows that toxic mold can germinate in 24 to 48 hours after a flood. If you have a mold problem, the cleanup has to be painstaking. If the problem is serious, you'll have to hire a professional, typically a firm with experience cleaning up after disasters such as floods and fires.

The sources of the mold have to be located, the areas have to be contained, and material removed under controlled circumstances. Then the areas must be vacuumed, washed, and vacuumed again. Drywall is porous, and if there's mold, it is all over the place. Hard furniture such as tables can be cleaned, but soft furniture such as couches has to be gotten rid of. Air tests must be taken before the job begins and after it is finished.

The basement is typically a site for mold growth. If the mold is extensive, it might require you to rip out everything down to the joists and studs and power wash the mold from the floors and walls. Then the surfaces have to be covered with several coats of waterproofing. Have the joists and studs inspected by a professional, typically a structural engineer. Because mold means that moisture is present, the lumber may not be able to dry completely and thus may be weakened and unable to support weight added during a renovation.

Still, if you removed everything that could contribute to mold growth in a house, you'd be left with the foundation and asphalt shingles on the roof. Unfortunately, everything that makes living in a house so pleasant for you is equally pleasant to the mold.

How do you know what to look for? A musty smell is one indi-
cation, but you need to check places on the top floor of your house
for a leaky roof as well for obvious signs such as discolored walls or
wet areas underneath sinks. If your walls show signs of mold (cracked/
peeling paint, bulging behind the paint, discoloration of walls), then
that section of drywall should be torn out and inspected.

The space between the wall and the baseboards serves as a great
growing ground for mold. Because it is a fairly sealed off space, it
traps moisture. Plus, a lot of dirt ends up here, providing the mold
colonies with plenty of nutrients to thrive. You'll have to get the situation under control before you begin any renovation project.

Remember, the way to control mold growth is to control moisture.
For example, you should repair leaky plumbing or problem roofs.
Keep an eye out for condensation and wet spots. You can prevent
moisture resulting from condensation by increasing surface temperatures or reducing moisture levels in the air. To increase the surface
temperature, insulate or increase the circulation of heated air. To reduce moisture levels in the air, repair leaks, increase ventilation (if
the outside air is cold and dry), or dehumidify (if outdoor air is warm
and humid).

A little maintenance is called for, including keeping heating,
ventilation, and air-conditioning (HVAC) drip pans clean, flowing
properly, and unobstructed. You also should vent moisture-generating
appliances, such as dryers, to the outside. By doing both, you'll be
better able to reach the recommended maximum indoor humidity of
60 percent, although it would be better if it ranged between 30 percent and 50 percent.

Don't allow the foundation of your house to remain wet. One
way to solve this problem is to provide adequate drainage by grad-
ing, or sloping the ground away from the house.

You need to find ways to increase ventilation so that the interior air
pressure is higher than the outside pressure, so that moisture and mold
flow out rather than in. Make sure that your heating, air-conditioning,
and ventilation system is properly sized for the house. When you add
on, you'll need to make sure that the size of the system grows to

accommodate it. When you add ductwork, have the existing duct-work cleaned.

31. THE AIR THAT WE BREATHE

Improving indoor air quality is money well spent.

■ ■ ■

As people age, they tend to develop allergies or reduced toler-ance to chemicals that they probably didn't even notice when they were younger. My wife is one of those people, and that has made me very careful about performing certain tasks around her, as well as ensuring that the contractors and repair people we employ take those precautions, too.

Here are a couple of examples. We ordered cabinets for one of our kitchen renovation projects. The boxes containing the cabinets arrived and sat in a pile in the foyer for a few days. My wife became ill about the same time. I moved the boxes to an area of the basement in which the floor joists had been insulated. My wife got well almost immediately. We assume that some chemical in the cardboard boxes was making her sick.

A few years later, we hired some painters to take care of a hall-way so I could get the house on the market to sell. The painters had been relatively sloppy, and my wife found a can of latex paint re-mover and began using it on the droppings of the floor. In about a half-hour, the odor of the chemical had overwhelmed her, and she al-most ended up in the emergency room.

You never know.

Our new house has a whole-house air cleaner, which also makes it virtually dust-free. The filter is changed every three months. The air cleaner seems to have made life for everyone with allergies in my house more tolerable and less dependent on antihistamines.

After exposure to all the chemicals that have become part of our daily existence, many people fall victim to something called "multiple chemical sensitivity," which means that just about everything around them makes them sick—from the kerosene-based ink used in newspapers, to the mold spores on the pages of books, to the outside air laden with automobile exhausts, to the fragrance designed to mask the soapy odor of dishwashing detergent.

Exposure to mold and other indoor pollutants does not create a problem for the inhabitants of a house in a day or a month but in two, three, or five years. The gradual introduction of time-weighted exposure to indoor pollutants causes problems. As buildings became tighter and less able to breathe, we also began spending more time indoors—working longer hours, spending more time with our families, needing security in a less secure world. Research indicates that people spend about 90 percent of their time indoors. Thus, for many, the risks to health may be greater because of exposure to air pollution indoors.

What is worse is that the people who might be affected most by indoor pollution often cannot escape their environment. These include the young and the elderly and, especially, the chronically ill suffering from respiratory or cardiovascular disease.

The government says that the primary causes of indoor air-quality problems are sources of pollution that release gas or particles into the air. Outdoor air must be brought into a house to dilute emissions and carry these pollutants outside, where they can dissipate. High temperatures and high levels of humidity also can increase the levels of pollutants. Sources of indoor pollution include combustion sources such as oil, gas, kerosene, coal, wood, and tobacco. Since the 1950s, residential builders have used more manufactured products in construction and remodeling. Plywood, adhesives, and a host of home furnishings such as carpets and drapes are manufactured with thousands of chemicals.

Air from the outdoors needed to dilute indoor pollution can enter a house three ways: infiltration (through cracks in the walls and joints in floors), natural ventilation (open doors and windows), and mechanical ventilation (outdoor-vented fans such as those in range hoods in kitchens and in bathrooms, as well as whole-house systems that remove indoor air and distribute filtered air through the house).

So, can central air-conditioning solve your moisture and ventilation problems? Most central air-conditioning systems are not sized properly for the house, and they do not run all the time, kicking in when they are needed. A better answer is to have a dehumidifier running from June to November. Be sure to clean the filter regularly and get rid of the water. Poorly maintained dehumidifiers can work against you.

The effects of indoor pollution can be experienced soon after exposure or years later. Immediate effects could include eye, nose, and throat irritation; headaches; dizziness; and fatigue. Immediate effects are short term and treatable, in most cases. Because most of us are not trained medical personnel, we often assume that we are sick for the wrong reasons. Studies in the 1990s, for example, showed that many people seeking emergency room treatment for prolonged respiratory illnesses in the winter actually were suffering from extended exposure to carbon monoxide caused by poorly maintained heating systems. When treated early, the effects of carbon monoxide exposure can be reversed. If not, the damage can be permanent.

In many cases, treatment is simply eliminating the person's exposure to the source of the pollution, if it can be identified. Symptoms of some diseases, including asthma, hypersensitivity pneumonitis, and humidifier fever, may also show up soon after exposure to some indoor air pollutants.

One's immediate reaction to indoor air pollutants depends on several factors. Age and preexisting medical conditions are two important influences. In other cases, whether someone reacts to a pollutant depends on individual sensitivity, which varies tremendously. Some people appear to become sensitized to biological and chemical pollutants after repeated exposures. Other health effects may show up years after exposure has occurred or only after long or repeated exposure.

You can deal with indoor pollution in a few different ways. One is to avoid pollutants by eliminating problems at the source, such as asking the only smoker in the house to take it outside. If you can't avoid pollutants, then you need to seal them out. Another way to get rid of pollution is to use some sort of mechanical ventilation system, such as kitchen or bathroom fan. Finally, you can use a whole-house air cleaner to filter out the pollutants.

An obvious way to reduce the concentration of indoor air pollutants is to increase the amount of outdoor air coming indoors. Opening windows and doors, operating window or attic fans, or running a window air conditioner with the vent control open increases the ventilation rate. New home designs are beginning to feature mechanical systems that bring outdoor air inside. Some designs include energy-efficient heat-recovery ventilators, also known as air-to-air heat exchangers. These can be adapted to older construction during the renovation process.

Many kinds of air cleaners are available, from room units to whole-house systems. These remove particulates but are not generally designed to remove gaseous pollutants. By controlling relative humidity in a home, the growth of some biological contaminants can be minimized. Relative humidity of 30 to 50 percent is generally recommended.

You can design your renovation projects to minimize indoor pollution, in consultation with your contractor and architect. Your local chapter of the American Lung Association (http://www.lungusa.org) has access to data obtained from the various "healthy house" efforts of its chapters around the country.

If your carpeting has been around for a while, it likely contains a variety of volatile organic compounds from adhesives, resins, and preservatives used in its manufacture. The level of such compounds in carpeting is not high, but if they make you dizzy or nauseous, that is a problem. The carpeting industry has recognized the problem and has reduced the use of formaldehyde in adhesives. Some smaller manufacturers are actually making area rugs of natural seaweed, while others are using nontoxic dyes.

If you are having your floors refinished, you should leave the house while the work is being done, owing to the dust and the odor of varnish. But water-based polyurethane that "off-gasses" quickly can be used to protect refinished floors, making them harmless to chemically sensitive people.

Likewise, modern paints are being formulated with low-volatile organic compounds. Paint odors also can be reduced by mixing baking soda with the paint before you apply it. The baking soda neutralizes the paint odor in the container and on the wall, just as it does with smelly carpets and refrigerators.

32. A FLICKER OF HOPE

Tackle the wiring first before you begin renovating.

■ ■ ■

Where were you when the lights went out?

If you live in an older home, you probably were using the vacuum cleaner, a hair dryer, and a computer on the same floor at the same time. The electrical systems of many old houses aren't designed to handle all of our newfangled appliances, so by trying to use all three at once, you probably blew a fuse or tripped a circuit breaker.

Just about every older house has more than one generation of electrical wiring, and homes that were built in the early 20th century, in the years after Thomas Edison flipped the switch to light lower Manhattan, can have four. What causes problems is perpetually tapping off the existing wiring to meet new electrical needs without upgrading the system. Because the kinds of appliances we buy today put demands on existing wiring that are greater than what the wiring was designed to handle, you have to update.

If you are planning even a minor renovation project that involves, say, the installation of lighting or electrical outlets, you have to be absolutely sure that there is enough available power for safe and uninterrupted operation. Ignoring electrical problems, or creating ones by overloading the system, can result in fire, serious injury, and death.

According to the Consumer Product Safety Commission (http://www.cspc.gov), 40,000 residential fires each year are attributable directly to problems with electrical wiring systems. These fires typically result in 350 deaths a year and cause thousands of injuries from electric shocks and burns, the commission says. They also cause more than $2 billion in personal property damage annually. Electrical cords and plugs were involved in about 7,100 of the 40,000 fires, directly causing 120 deaths, or almost one-third of the total, the commission reported.

Although homeowners can check for faults in their electrical service and come up with things that need to be updated and improved, the best person to handle the changes is a licensed electrician. There are a number of ways to find a qualified electrician, including recommendations from friends, relatives, and neighbors. A growing number of consumers are finding contractors on Web sites that list only those individuals and companies with credentials that pass rigorous examination.

Don't try tackling electrical work yourself, even if you are a top-of-the-line do-it-yourselfer. Many municipalities require permits for substantial—and, in some cases, minor—changes in home electrical wiring such as adding an outlet or running a separate line to a junction box for a ceiling fan. Building officials often will not approve any work unless it has been performed, or at least examined, by a licensed professional.

According to home inspectors, the primary cause of problems with electrical systems is that the work was done by the homeowner or by an unqualified moonlighter who may have been inexpensive but wasn't very good. Going this route might save you money now, but it will definitely cost you more in time and aggravation. In addition, such work can go up in smoke.

Although most consumers aren't qualified to be electricians, that doesn't mean you shouldn't learn as much as you can about how the system works. Plenty of books and videos on the subject are available at bookstores and home centers. While some of these take a textbook, rather than commonsense, approach that will leave most electricians puzzled or laughing hysterically, most handle the basics very well.

Each year, there are changes to the National Electrical Code that, while not yet adopted by local building departments, might affect how an inspector will look at your wiring in the future. Be sure your electrician is up on the rules.

The utility company is responsible for the line that runs from the light pole on the street up to and including the splices on top of the service head, as well as the meter, which it owns. So the electrician should begin analyzing your service at the panel box in the basement. One of the first things the electrician should make sure of is that the branch circuits from the box to the different parts of the house have circuit breakers that are sized properly. The box also should be grounded properly. Grounding is normally done when you install a new 100-amp service. In older homes, the box was grounded to the copper cold-water pipes, but because newer homes have polyvinyl chloride (PVC) pipes, a ground rod is required.

In analyzing a home's system, an electrician should make sure that all the branch circuits are in good shape and that all the splices have been made properly. Many homeowners are installing 200-amp service to accommodate more of those newfangled appliances. While experts debate whether 100 amps are too little or 200 amps too much, a 100-amp service typically meets the needs of a house with 1,500 to 2,500 square feet of space. A 200-amp service panel gives you more power, but not on each branch circuit. Fifteen amps are still 15 amps. What is important is not the amount of amperage, but the way it is distributed.

The electrician should also analyze the wiring as part of the job. The oldest wiring in an old house is knob and tube, installed between 1900 and 1910. Two wires, insulated with rubberized cloth run independently of each other along beams from the basement through the center of the house. Where they run through the joists, they are encased in ceramic tubes to prevent the wire from chafing on the wood. The wires that run over joists are looped around ceramic knobs nailed to the joists—hence knob and tube. Usually, four branch circuits are soldered to the two wires, and each circuit is carried to a part of the house.

The succeeding generations of wiring are BX, a metal-clad armored cable; the original Romex (two wires encased in rubberized cloth cable); and modern Romex, with hot, neutral, and safety-ground wires encased in heavy plastic insulation. Knob-and-tube wiring, being the oldest, should be looked at the most closely. The electrician might not need to tear it out but should rewire areas where power use is the heaviest.

In a complete kitchen renovation, all new branch circuits should be installed and old ones disconnected. Most kitchen appliances require their own circuits. Bathrooms should have circuits of 15 to 20 amps per receptacle to handle hairdryers and similar appliances. Bathrooms, kitchens, and normally damp areas such as basements, garages, crawlspaces, and the outdoors should have outlets known as ground-fault circuit interrupters, or GFCIs, which halt the electricity supply immediately if the outlet comes into contact with moisture.

GFCIs constantly monitor electricity flowing in a circuit. If the electricity flowing into the circuit differs by even a slight amount from that returning, the GFCI will quickly shut off the current flowing through that circuit. The advantage of using GFCIs is that they can detect even small variations in the amount of leakage current, even amounts too small to activate a fuse or circuit breaker. GFCIs work quickly, so they can help protect consumers from severe electric shocks and electrocution.

Personal computers should be on a new, grounded circuit. And if the electrician is running new electrical wire anywhere in the house, he should be simultaneously adding Category 5 cable that carries phone and Internet data, coaxial cable for audio and video signals, and speaker wire to each room.

If ceiling fans or lighting fixtures are being installed, so should new junction boxes. In the knob and tube days, a junction box was just a piece of wood with two holes drilled in it. Most have become unsafe. Older ceiling fixtures encapsulate the heat produced by those fixtures, and the trapped heat bakes the wires, like one of those Suzy Homemaker ovens that used a light bulb to bake a cake. The insulation becomes brittle and breaks. Nine out of ten times, the fixture stops working. The tenth time, it could start a fire. To fix the problem, the electrician takes out the brittle wire, makes a new splice, and installs a junction box. If rewiring the room, the electrician takes the new wire through a switch and then to the junction box.

Some homes built in the 1960s and 1970s have aluminum wire because it was cheaper than copper. As long as the wire has been installed properly and is connected to switches and receptacles designed for it, don't tear it out. As long the electrician is there anyway, however, maybe you should have it replaced.

33. CLOSING THE GAPS

All old houses are poorly insulated.

■ ■ ■

Here's a simple, somewhat reliable test of whether your house is adequately insulated.

On a cloudy day when the furnace or central air-conditioning is off, put a thermometer on a chair in the middle of a room with at least one exterior wall. Then tape another thermometer to that wall, and wait a few minutes. If the temperature in the middle of the room is within a few degrees of the reading on the wall thermometer, then the insulation in that wall at least is good enough. But if there is a big difference between the two, it may be time to make some changes.

Heating and cooling account for 50 percent to 70 percent of the energy used in the typical American home, according to the federal Department of Energy (http://www.doe.gov), which also estimates that 20 percent goes for heating water, while 10 to 30 percent is consumed by lighting, appliances, and everything else. Insulation can do much to lower your utility bills in summer as well as winter. Properly done, whether by a professional installer or the homeowner, it can make life extremely comfortable when the weather outside is not.

If you need a more professional reckoning of your needs, you can have an energy audit performed. Some utility companies offer such audits free, while professionals can charge up to $500 for them. Check the Web site of the National Association of Energy Service Companies (http://www.naesco.org) for a list of experts in your area.

A professional audit should be a detailed room-by-room analysis, including a blower-door test and a thermographic scan. The Energy Department explains the methods this way. A blower door is a fan mounted into an exterior doorframe. The fan pulls air out of the house, lowering the air pressure inside. The higher outside air pressure then flows in through all unsealed cracks and openings. Thermography, or infrared scanning, measures surface temperatures with video and still cameras, which record the temperature variations of the building's skin. The tests are designed to check for air leaks and to determine where insulation should be installed, or whether what is already there was put in improperly.

If your house is not insulated, see whether insulation would help cut the heat loss. If it has insulation, it might not be enough to meet federal recommendations. For example, if you have less than 11 to 12 inches of attic insulation, you probably need more.

Because heat is a form of energy, it always seeks a cooler area, flowing out of the house in winter and into the house in summer. Insulation reduces the heat flow, and, when used properly, it results in using less energy for heating and cooling. How well insulation resists heat flow is its R-value. Standard fiberglass insulation is rated at R-3.5 per inch. R-11, recommended for exterior walls, is about 3.5 inches. R-38, used for ceilings below ventilated attics, is about 13 inches thick. The first inch offers the most resistance to heat escape; each consecutive inch offers slightly less.

R-values are cumulative, so there is no need to remove what's already there. By layering two different batts together, you get the combined R-value of both batts. For example, two layers of R-19 batts will give you a total of R-38.

Fiberglass insulation is found in many older and new homes, ranging from R-11 to R-38. In attics, rolls of fiberglass insulation that come without paper or foil facing are laid on top of one another to reach the recommended R value. Mineral wool insulation is made from hard slag and spun like fiberglass and has the same R-value as fiberglass. Cellulose fill is made from newspapers, treated with fire retardant, and can be poured or blown into wall cavities. Extruded polystyrene, or rigid-board insulation, has an R-value of 5 per inch. Expanded polystyrene is rated R-3.5 per inch.

Polyurethane is a yellowish or white foam with an R-value of 6 per inch. On the consumer level, it comes in a spray can with a plastic tube that can be inserted into the aerosol sprayer for more accurate application. It bubbles after application and can be trimmed. Polyisocyanurate is a plastic with an R-value of 6.3 per inch. It is often backed with foil to reflect radiant heat. Bubble pack looks like packing material attached to foil. It also acts as a vapor barrier. House wrap is used in renovation jobs in which additions are created or existing siding is replaced. It is installed with staples over the wood sheathing and allows interior moisture to escape while preventing air filtration around windows and doors.

The facing material on the insulation is generally a vapor barrier. It is usually applied toward the "warm-in-winter" portion of the house to help resist the movement of moisture vapor to cold surfaces, where it can condense. This means that, in the ceilings, the barrier faces down; in the walls, it faces the inside; and in the floors over unheated spaces, it faces up.

Insulation does its job best when it is used in the right amount and in the right places. This means insulating the attic to the recommended level, including the attic door or hatch cover. In addition, use the recommended level of insulation under floors above unheated spaces, around walls in a heated basement or unventilated crawl space, and on the edges of slabs on grade.

Use the recommended levels of insulation for exterior walls for new-house construction (R-18) when remodeling or residing your house. Consider using new-construction levels in your existing walls. The overall R-value of a wall or ceiling will be somewhat different from that of the insulation itself, because some heat flows around the insulation through the studs and joists. That is, the overall R-value of a wall with insulation between wood studs is less than the R-value of the insulation itself, because the wood provides what is called a "thermal short-circuit" around the insulation. Short-circuiting through metal framing is much greater than that through wood-framed walls; sometimes, a metal wall's overall R-value can be as low as half the insulation's R-value, Energy Department experts say.

Whether you should install insulation yourself depends on the structural design of your house and the type of materials used in its construction. Installing it yourself does save money if done correctly, and often insulation contractors are overscheduled, so you might not be able to hire one when you need one.

Placing insulation in an attic floor is usually easy, requiring laying the material between the parallel joists of the frame. Be careful not to step through the joists, or you'll have a foot through the ceiling below. You have to seal air leaks between your living space and the attic before adding insulation. Insulation placed between joists, rafters, and studs does not retard heat flow, called thermal bridging, through the exposed frame. In attics, thermal bridging can be reduced by adding sufficient loose-fill insulation, or cross-installed batts, to cover the frame.

In existing buildings, installing insulation in the cavity of exterior walls is difficult. It usually requires the services of a contractor with equipment for blowing loose-fill insulation into the cavity through small holes cut through the side wall. The holes are closed later. Rigid insulation can be installed on the outside of concrete block or poured concrete walls. That also goes for basement or crawl-space walls, or floors over unheated areas, using rigid insulation or batt insulation.

If you insulate a floor above a crawl space, all ducts and water lines running below the insulation should be insulated as well. Insulate crawl-space walls only if the space is dry all year, the floor above is not insulated, all ventilation to the crawl space is blocked, and a vapor barrier (heavy polyethylene sheets) is installed on the ground to reduce moisture coming in.

34. PLUMBING THE DEPTHS

What's behind the walls may cost you big bucks.

■ ■ ■

Every older house has its share of plumbing woes, but let me share a story about new houses to illustrate that *new* doesn't always mean *problem-free*. It also illustrates why you should bring in professionals before you buy a house and maintain a list of reliable contractors and repair people after you buy.

A doctor bought a $500,000 luxury home in a development that is known in the residential construction business as a "workout." What this means is that the original developer had gotten into financial trouble and the bank had foreclosed and found a second developer to finish the project. The second developer, as many major builders do, employs an army of subcontractors. The company employed to connect the houses to the sewer lines made the connections, and the work was inspected by the local building official. The lines were buried, grass was planted, and buyers came.

The doctor and his family moved into their new house two days before Christmas. On Christmas Eve, the doctor went to use the bathroom sink. It clogged. He then went to use the toilet. It jammed. The dishwasher was running, and water and suds began coming up through the adjacent sink drain, running over the floor until he was able to shut the machine down.

The bottom line: The subcontractors had connected the houses to a sewer line that the first developer had started but never finished. It was long enough to handle 24 hours worth of sewage, but after that, the waste had nowhere to go but back.

The result: Unhappy holidays. Drawn out battles ensued with the homeowners insurance company and with the second developer, who played a game of "we have more lawyers than you do," until the doctor threatened to bring the story to the media.

A lot of uncertainty hides behind the walls of your house. Hidden problems have hidden costs, and can delay the start and certainly the completion of any remodeling job that involves plumbing.

I've dealt with any number of these problems over the years. The most recent was when I had our master bath remodeled to add a tub and extend the tile floor. When the plumber began laying the water and drain lines for the tub, he discovered that the water supply lines were one-quarter inch instead of half-inch or three-quarters of an inch in diameter. They were not only inadequate but did not meet building code.

A worse, and more common, problem was that the existing drain lines from the double shower and bathroom sink to the soil stack were inadequately sloped. The 2½-inch drains should have been sloped one-quarter-inch per foot to allow waste water to move at slow enough rate of speed to carry solids along but quickly enough to scrape the walls of the pipe.

Correcting these two problems added $2,900 to the job and included creating false beams in the ceiling below the master bath to allow the pipes to slope properly.

Another major problem is a clogged soil line, which can prevent sewage from traveling uninterrupted to the sewer or the septic tank. The reasons for the blockage are virtually endless. Tree roots can wrap themselves around the buried pipe and crack it. Age can take its toll. Of course, homeowners can dump things into the drains that don't belong in them. These can include tree branches (a homeowner once used the garbage disposal to chop one up), clumps of paper towels (they aren't as biodegradable as toilet paper or tissues and tend to wad into a ball), and feminine napkins. The warning on the box says that these sanitary products should not be flushed down toilets in houses with septic systems, but it says nothing about older houses with sewer lines. You may not do it, but if the last two homeowners did, you'll end up paying for the problem.

Well, maybe not. We paid for previous owners' abuse of our soil pipe, and the sewer service repairman showed us the clumps of sanitary napkins that caused it. Our plumber, Marcel Paillard, who had recommended the sewer cleaner, suggested that I write to the maker of the sanitary napkins and see if I could get the cost of the cleanout reimbursed. I sent a letter and a copy of the invoice. I received a check for the full amount.

Clearing the soil line of any blockage can be costly, depending on how long it takes to find and clear the obstruction. The sewer cleaning company often will not guarantee the work after the line has been cleared, if it suspects that abuses that created the problem will continue.

Cleanouts on all drains have to be easily accessible. And water supply lines on all fixtures should have working shut-off valves. Paillard recommends that, because toilets tend to jam more often than other fixtures, you should insist that such a valve be installed.

When sink and tub drains show signs of running slowly, you need to tackle the problem before it gets expensive to solve. Slow drainage can be usually traced to accumulation of soap, hair, or food. Keep a plunger on hand.

Septic tanks should be inspected annually and cleaned every two to three years, or whenever necessary. They also may need to be replaced or expanded if you add a bathroom or improve a kitchen. How can you anticipate septic tank problems? If the area above the absorption field is growing greener grass than surrounding areas, then you may have some flooding in the absorption area, indicating inadequate drainage.

In the past, it was unthinkable to install a garbage disposal in a house with a septic system. Having one would double the amount of solids being disposed of, requiring you to have the tank pumped out twice as often. However, In-Sink-Erator, a garbage disposal manufacturer, introduced a model designed for use with septic tanks that costs about $300. The secret: Bio-Charge®, a solution filled with natural microorganisms injected into the grind chamber every time the disposal is activated, which breaks down food waste.

Another thing you'll have to look at when renovating is whether the hot water heater is adequate to meet additional needs. Making this decision would be easier, of course, if the hot water heater was old and needed replacing. However, because storage hot water heaters can last as long as 25 years if maintained properly, you might be better off adding a second heater and zoning the two of them. For example, one 40-gallon heater might serve the kitchen, the first floor bathroom, and the hot tub, while the second would feed the rest of the house.

In most cases, a 50-gallon electric water heater or a 40-gallon gas water heater is appropriate. Gas heats water faster, so it can be smaller than the electric model. If you have gas, stay with gas. If you have electric and can convert to gas, then do it. Tankless water heaters will be discussed in a subsequent chapter.

You may want to look into solar water heaters, which cost more than gas and electric storage heaters but can actually save money over the long term, because the energy they depend on is free. The municipality may have something to say about placement of the solar collectors needed to heat the water. You'll likely need a backup if the solar heater doesn't provide enough hot water for all your needs.

One thing you'll have to think about is upgrading the plumbing in your house to meet modern needs. As with electrical wiring, you are likely to find several generations of plumbing, much of which is antiquated and probably poorly executed. If anything, much of it is not up to code and should be replaced before you embark on any updating projects.

For example, is there too much water pressure or not enough? Is the water meter functioning properly, or should it be replaced to reflect accurately how much water you are consuming? Are the water lines in good shape? Is the soil stack behind the walls that feed into the basement soil line developing cracks? Are fixtures properly vented? Is the toilet running constantly, or do you have dripping faucets? Both waste lots of water. Consider ways to conserve water. Look for places in your renovation plans where use can be reduced by installing water-saving showerheads and faucets.

35. RUNNING HOT AND COLD

Comfort will cost you, but it's worth the money.

■ ■ ■

If you are planning an addition, you'll probably have to make appropriate adjustments to your heating and air-conditioning systems. You'll notice that I didn't mention increasing the size of your heating and air-conditioning system. Proper sizing involves more than the square footage. It is also based on the amount of heat your house loses during cold weather and gains during warm weather.

Because heating and cooling systems are big-ticket items, we probably hang on to them longer than we should. While we are hanging on, technology improves, and the newer systems become much more energy efficient, and less expensive to operate, than the ones we are trying to save. In the long run, therefore, we lose money, not save it.

Every year, millions of American homeowners lose money in this way. Of the 43 million residential oil and gas furnaces in operation in U.S. homes, one in four is more than 20 years old. Many new furnaces are 25 percent to 40 percent more efficient than older ones. For example, the Energy Star program of the Environmental Protection Agency (http://www.epa.gov) promotes furnaces using a "condensing technology" as the most efficient. An efficiency rating tells you how much of the total energy used is delivered to the home as heat: the higher the rating, the better. A furnace that is 80 percent efficient delivers 80 percent of the fuel consumed to the house. The rest, 20 percent, is lost up the flue. Your heating bill, therefore, depends on the unit cost of fuel and on the efficiency of the furnace.

Gas condensing furnaces are considered the most efficient—between 90 and 96 percent efficient. The combustion gases in the furnace are cooled to the point where water vapor condenses, releasing additional heat into the house. The liquids that result are piped to a floor drain. Because the temperature of the flue gas is low, plastic pipes are used to vent the furnace out the sidewall of the house rather than through a conventional chimney. These furnaces tend to be slightly more efficient when they are run for shorter periods.

The cost of a new furnace can run from $1,200 to $12,000, depending on the size of the house and the kind of heating system being installed. Your heating contractor should not install a furnace with a higher capacity than needed for your house. Furnace manufacturers do not recommend oversizing furnaces, because the heating units will rust out and break down more often and cause the occupants more discomfort. Oversizing will shorten the life of the equipment by causing it to cycle on and off more frequently than a properly sized unit. An oversized furnace also will not run long enough and will have a long span between cycles—hence the "isn't it getting chilly in here at night" syndrome. Oversized equipment can also cause excessive air noise. On the other hand, undersized equipment, with airflow that is too low, can reduce the efficiency of the air distribution and accelerate wear on system components, leading to earlier failure.

A contractor who follows standards established by the American Society of Heating, Refrigerating, and Air-Conditioning Engineers (http://www.ashrae.org) will use a number of criteria to determine the proper size of your new furnace or central air-conditioning system. These include the exact square footage of your house, the amount of insulation in the walls and attic, and the number and condition of windows and doors. One important factor in the equation is your comfort level, which focuses on how you feel when you are sitting in the living room and the temperature outside is either 10 degrees or 90 degrees. By determining what you consider comfortable, the contractor will factor into the calculations the rooms that are uncomfortable in the winter or summer.

High-efficiency systems reduce fuel bills but are typically costlier up front than conventional ones. For furnaces, the experts say that heat load and fuel price should help you decide whether to go high-efficiency or conventional. *Heat load* refers to how much heat is typically used. It depends on size, how well the house is insulated, thermostat settings, and outside climate. You can get a rough estimate of heat load by looking at fuel bills. The higher the load and fuel bills, the easier it is to justify buying a high-efficiency system.

Even if the system is properly sized for your house, you could be losing money through a system that isn't balanced between the amount of air supplied to a room and the air returned to the air-conditioning unit or the furnace. The higher one goes in a house, the less efficient the heating or air-conditioning seems to be. A major reason is that not enough air on the upper floors is being returned to the basement or where the units are located. A return duct system can be added sometimes to balance the system.

Central air-conditioners, heat pumps, and forced air furnaces rely on a system of ducts to circulate air throughout your home. It's common to find gaps between duct joints. You should have the ducts sealed and insulated to improve comfort and efficiency. Leaky ducts also can cause an unbalanced system that wastes energy, 7 to 12 percent of the heating and cooling energy used by your home.

Houses with radiators and steam heat systems can be fitted for central air-conditioning without having to incur the cost of installing ductwork and tearing through walls and floors to do it. The solution: A system that uses small diameter, flexible ductwork threaded through closets and floor and ceiling joists to carry a high velocity stream of air to round outlets in the ceiling of each room. Air handlers and coils can be installed in ceilings, closets, or attic spaces.

Another option is radiant floor heating. In a radiant floor or hydronic heating system, heated water, circulating through plastic tubes under the floor, behaves just like a radiator, transferring heat uniformly from the floor to the objects above it. The basic principle of radiant heating is to control heat loss from the body as opposed to heat loss from the building. Skin-surface temperature, about 85 degrees, is generally warmer than the surrounding surfaces. The warm water in a radiant-floor system can be generated by a hot-water heater or existing hydronic equipment—hot-water baseboard or radiator. Or it can come from a new gas-fired or oil-fired boiler. Energy savings generated by the system—proponents say typically 30 percent—is achieved by not having to heat the water higher than 85 to 95 degrees. With proper design, radiant floor heating means that the house can be kept at a constant 66 degrees. That would be the same as keeping the thermostat in a forced-air system at 72 degrees.

Maintaining a consistent temperature requires the use of an indoor-outdoor boiler-reset control. An outdoor thermostat senses the outside air temperature. The indoor thermostat monitors the temperature of the circulating water in the floor. Those two temperatures are fed into a computer that varies the speed of the pump injecting the water from the boiler into the tubing.

Every time the temperature outdoors drops ten degrees, there is a corresponding ten-degree increase in the temperature of the circulating water. It is like the cruise control in a car. Enough heat is applied to compensate for the difference, but no more.

36. WHAT'S BUGGING YOU?

If you have termites, get rid of them before you start
your renovation project.

■ ■ ■

I've devoted Part 3 to driving home the point that, no matter how eager you are to make your house prettier, you have to take care of the ugly stuff first: inadequate heating, bad wiring, a worn-out roof, improper ventilation, and dangers to health such as radon, asbestos, and lead-based paint.

You want to talk really ugly? Let's talk about termites, which I had to deal with when I first got it into my head to renovate my first house 22 years ago. Squirrels are also ugly, especially when they find their way into your house through rotted fascia boards in the late fall and then spend the winter running back and forth along the joists in the ceiling above your bed in the middle of the night.

Do I have issues? You bet I have issues. And I won't even get into the theory that mice travel in nation states, not pairs or families.

Our first house, built in 1848, had an L-shaped structure added sometime in the 1920s so that the kitchen could be brought up from the basement to the first floor. Along the way, the long part of the L was divided into a bathroom and a laundry room. On the other side of the bathroom was a storage shed, attached to both the exterior wall and to a cement block wall. The storage shed was rotted out, and I decided to demolish it. Just as began my work in the early spring, a great quantity of bugs began swarming around me. I had seen them before, in the backyard of one of my parents' houses. We had a termite infestation, with food provided by a rotted shed and years of deferred maintenance.

We bought the house in March 1982. In those days, lenders insisted on termite reports as a condition of obtaining a mortgage. We had a termite inspection that said that the house was clean and came with a year's guarantee. I began demolishing the shed in April 1983, and that's when the termites appeared. My question is: How did the termites know that the guarantee was up?

We called an exterminator who confirmed that we had termites, and for $500 and a five-year warranty, the technician drilled holes in the concrete along the perimeter of the house and injected them with chlordane, a now-banned chemical treatment, designed to keep the beasts away from the foundation and directed instead toward your neighbors' houses, unless they've had treatments, too.

In most states, termite inspections these days are contingencies in agreements of sale, with the lenders leaving execution up to real estate agents. These sales agreements have what are known as wood-infestation clauses, covering termites, carpenter ants, and other wood-boring insects. If evidence of termite infestation is found, the seller is required to pay to have the problem treated. The repair of the damage is then negotiated between the buyer and the seller. Usually the buyer will only walk away from the deal if the seller will not take care of the damage, which often can run into thousands of dollars.

Fortunately, the damage to my home was limited to something I was removing anyway, but, even so, the problem needed to be tackled before any renovation could be carried out. In this case, we had an L-shaped addition, covered with asphalt shingles as was common in the 1950s, coated instead with stucco, because the rest of the house was brick. We couldn't afford brick and complete the rest of the renovations we wanted, so stucco was the compromise.

Although it is dangerous to generalize, most real estate agents suggest that termite infestation is more common in houses more than ten years old. An important reason is that foundation construction methods have changed in the last decade to reduce the likelihood of termite damage. If you are considering an addition, you should ask your contractor to look into these new methods to ensure that you won't have to be spending big bucks on repairs and treating termite infestation a few years down the road.

Termite infestation requires wood from a structure to come directly in contact with the soil. What builders have started doing is constructing termite barriers to prevent such contact. One barrier is made of stone and looks like very coarse, sharp sand. Granite is crushed and graded to a specific size and shape of particle. These particles are too big for termites to move, too small for them to go between, too hard to chew, and too sharp to push through. They are then packed into all the termite-entry points of a new building—for example, exterior perimeter wall cavities and pipes through slabs.

Termites use their jaws rather than their legs to move forward. Tests of termite barriers show that the creatures are unable to move particles larger than about 1 millimeter in diameter. As particle size increases, so does the size of the space between the particles. Particles about 3 millimeters and larger provide spaces large enough for termites to crawl through. Therefore, coarse sand particles—which range from 1 to 3 millimeters—can be used as a barrier around the foundation of a house to protect against subterranean termites. Sand barriers can also be used in perimeter trenches and crawl spaces, inside hollow masonry voids, and around the bases of fence posts, poles, supporting piers, porches, decks, and retaining walls.

Another barrier is made of a noncorroding, stainless steel mesh. The gaps in the mesh are small enough to prevent penetration by termites. This barrier is used with slab-on-grade construction by placing it on the aggregate bed before pouring the concrete floor pad.

Termite inspections are typically conducted by licensed inspectors, either independent contractors or franchisees of larger firms. An inspection usually takes an hour to 90 minutes, depending on the size of the house. One problem is that inspectors cannot report on what they cannot see, so their written determinations include exceptions to areas that are not accessible. In fact, about 80 percent of the wood in a typical house is hidden from view.

Fairly obvious signs of termite infestation that even the layperson can see include pencil-thin mud tubes extending over the inside and outside surfaces of foundation walls, piers, sills, and joists; the presence of winged termites or their shed wings on windowsills and along the edges of floors; and damaged wood hollowed out along the grain and lined with bits of mud or soil. The inspector's trained eye can see other, more subtle evidence.

The inspector is looking first for any signs of an active infestation, which include any shelter or mud tubes constructed by subterranean termites on or in a wall that enables the termites to gain access to wooden construction elements from their colony beneath the soil. The use of a moisture meter is invaluable in these inspections, because it can reveal areas behind the walls with a high moisture content. This moisture can be indicative of a plumbing leak, water from a sprinkler system, or a roof leak. These all contribute to conditions conducive to infestation by termites, as subterranean termites can use the moisture for survival.

In these instances, an opening may need to be made in the wall to determine if the moisture is simply from some leak and if it is encouraging a termite infestation. Inspectors also will use a flashlight, probes, and powers of observation to determine the presence of an infestation. They will inspect inside the structure, outside the structure, beneath the structure if there is a pier-and-beam foundation, and in the attic.

Pest control operators use several different insecticides. All are safe and effective when used carefully according to label directions and will remain effective in the soil for five to ten years. The second option is termite bait, which consists of a food material that termites like combined with a very slow-acting toxic substance. Baiting is a slow, long-term solution to a termite problem. A comprehensive baiting program seeks to maintain a termite-free condition through ongoing monitoring and rebaiting as needed. Many professional pest control companies use termite baits as well as insecticides to keep termite colonies under control.

■ THINGS TO REMEMBER

55. Before you renovate, check for health hazards such as asbestos, lead-based paint, and radon. They should be dealt with before the contractor begins disturbing the fabric of the house.

56. As much as 70 percent of a home's heat can be lost through lack of insulation.

57. Attics with a ceiling vapor barrier must be ventilated with at least one square foot of vent area for each 300 square feet of ceiling.

58. Insurers won't include coverage of mold damage in standard policies written in 43 states.

59. Not every mold is a potential hazard. Some people, however, are more sensitive to mold than others.

60. The way to control mold growth is to control moisture.

61. Many people who visit hospital emergency rooms for treatment of prolonged respiratory illnesses in the winter actually suffer from extended exposure to carbon monoxide poisoning from badly maintained heating systems.

62. Indoor relative humidity of 30 to 50 percent should be your goal.

63. When buying paints and carpeting, or sealing wood floors after refinishing, choose products formulated with low-volatility organic compounds.

64. Forty thousand residential fires annually are attributed to electrical system problems.

65. Most kitchen appliances require their own electrical circuits.

66. Ground fault interrupter circuit (GFIC) outlets should be installed in normally damp areas to reduce the risk of electrical shock.

67. To see if you need to correct insulation problems as part of your renovation, obtain a room-to-room professional energy audit, including a blower-door test and thermographic scan.

68. Tackle slow-draining sinks before they need to be professionally cleaned.

69. Don't use your plumbing fixtures for anything they weren't designed to handle, such as grinding tree branches in your garbage disposal.

70. When adding to your house, consider upgrading your older heating and cooling system to a modern, energy-saving model.

71. Get a system properly sized for your house. Oversizing can reduce comfort and shorten the life of the equipment by causing it to cycle on and off more frequently.

72. Heat load and fuel price should determine whether you go with a high-efficiency system or a conventional one.

73. Older houses can be fitted with air-conditioning without costly ductwork installation.

74. Consider radiant floor heating, which can save up to 30 percent on energy bills.

75. Seal your ductwork. Leaky ducts can waste 7 to 12 percent of your heating and cooling energy.

PART 4

THE GOOD, THE BAD, AND THE UGLY

. . .

The last section looks at some of the renovation projects that can add value to your house as well as those that might not. I say some, but not all. Had I included every project that I thought would be appropriate for this section, this book would weigh a couple of thousand pounds, and you'd need a truck to haul it home from the bookstore.

I tried to focus on the projects that, over the years, my readers have asked me about most often, or ones that I've found bring the most feedback when I write about them. It's all subjective, really. I know I am not making any friends among the pool and spa industry, but experience has shown that not everyone wants a pool. Home office designers won't like me either, but I believe that workspaces should be functional first and pretty second, or even third.

The best advice I can offer is: when in doubt, pick a color and buy a can of paint. It can transform the saddest-looking space into a work of art. I know. I just spent $40 on paint and turned a dingy basement into a place people are willing to congregate. I said $40, not $40,000.

If you have a house that can accommodate one, add a fireplace, especially a virtually maintenance-free gas one. Nothing is nicer than arriving home at dusk on a damp, chilly winter's day and clicking a remote control to light the fireplace.

If I could only find a place for a laundry room on the second floor, life would be perfect. But, as you'll see in Chapter 39 about low-flow toilets, life never is.

37. YOU CAN LIVE HERE ALMOST FOREVER

Consider making your renovation project barrier-free.

■ ■ ■

My late father-in-law, Thomas M. Gray, spent most of his life being active. He played semiprofessional hockey in his teens. He and his father would swim across the East River between Brooklyn and Manhattan, or so family legend says. He spent many years as a coach, first of sandlot baseball and his daughters' soccer. He also was an avid gardener, do-it-yourselfer, and woodworker. Most importantly, he was a father to seven children, all of whom achieved great success in their various fields.

At 57, he discovered that he had diabetes. By the time he reached his late 60s, the disease, and a fall in which he broke a hip that could not be repaired, left him wheelchair-bound. He slept on a daybed in the family room of his two-story house for the last four years of his life, unable to get to his second-floor bedroom. The first-floor bathroom had no shower. Each day, he'd struggled to shave and clean up seated in his wheelchair, prevented from getting close to the sink by the vanity. A makeshift ramp of pressure-treated wood from the kitchen door through the garage helped him get to the car by wheelchair for doctor visits.

This was not the way he wanted to spend his last years, nor do any of us want this. But things happen, and the only way we can deal with such health-related problems is to prepare for them in advance.

In response to growing demand, the National Association of Home Builders (http://www.nahb.org), the National Multi Housing Council (http://www.nmhc.org), the Remodelors Council (http://www.nahb.org), and advocacy organizations for people with disabilities have been developing barrier-free housing that falls into the "universal design" category. *Universal design* incorporates most federal design and accessibility guidelines because, over time, it allows a consumer to grow into a house. Making the house entirely wheelchair accessible by designing wider hallways and entryways is a way to avoid costly retrofitting later.

The philosophy behind barrier-free housing takes two trends into account. One is that people 45 and older buying trade-up housing don't plan to move every seven years, long the national average. The other is that, as people age, they will progressively have trouble doing everyday tasks, such as reaching down to open a kitchen drawer, reaching up to get a book on the top shelf of the bookcase, or stepping over the raised base of a shower stall without having something to grab onto.

Universal-design features make the house accessible to everyone, not just those having increasing problems with accessibility. Features include front-loading washers and dryers, ovens with side hinges, and electrical outlets that the homeowner can use without getting down on their hands and knees. It also includes lever-handle door and faucet hardware throughout the house, recessed door fronts on base cabinets for wheelchair access to sinks, a staircase that can easily be retrofitted for a chair lift, and a no-threshold shower in the master bath.

If you are building an addition, try to limit the number of hallways that might hamper accessibility, and throw the space you save into enlarging the bathroom, for example. A 5-by-5 shower provides plenty of room for a patient and an aide, and accessibility can be achieved with a ramp. A 5-by-5 space around the toilet area also will provide enough room for a wheelchair-bound person to use the facilities easily.

Some houses include flexible "bonus" space that can accommodate a live-in nurse if that becomes necessary. An addition can include first-floor space that can be converted into a bedroom later or a master bedroom now, thus shifting guestrooms to the second floor. That way, a wheelchair-bound homeowner can have easy access to the outdoors. All doorways inside and out should be designed to accommodate a wheelchair and someone pushing it. The cabinet below a cook top should be removable so someone in a wheelchair can cook there.

Improved medical care has helped make middle age halfway to 100 years, and because we are healthier at 50 or 60 than our grandparents or parents, we don't like to confront universal design, even though we know that if we do it now, we won't have to worry about it later. You can get the contractor to frame your new bathroom to accommodate grab bars in the shower, tub, and near the toilet for future installation. Doorways can be made 30 inches wide to accommodate wheelchairs without making a big deal of it. The kitchen can be made accessible for wheelchairs. Nine-foot windows that let in more light can be as much an architectural feature as an aid to people with failing eyesight down the road.

Almost 20 percent of the population has some level of disability, and 10 percent describe the disability as severe, according to the Census Bureau (http://www.census.gov). The vast majority of those are adults 45 years and older, the same group that will be the chief consumer of trade-up housing for at least the next 20 years, according to the National Association of Home Builders.

While statistics show that the demand for accessible housing is growing, many remodeling contractors might argue that such changes are costly and that first-floor master suites and ramps, for example, will affect resale. Don't believe it. Remember that such changes will allow you to live in your house for a very long time. Universal design features will likely be more cost-effective and less of a disruption in your life than buying a new house designed to be free of barriers.

One positive development has been the recent proliferation of companies that produce household items designed to make life easier for the disabled. These include electronic-sensor faucets, built-in seats in showers, and motorized scooters.

It is, of course, true that new houses are easier to make barrier-free than older ones. The California Foundation for Independent Living Centers (http://www.cfilc.org) said that a zero-step entry for a new house costs $150—about a third of the price of a bay window—

while wider interior doors cost $50. To retrofit older houses, conservative estimates of the cost of a zero-step entrance is $1,000, while widening an existing doorway is as much as $700, according to estimates supplied to the foundation by the National Association of Home Builders. That's why, if you are planning an addition, it is wise to make it barrier-free and inclusive enough to accommodate a wheelchair-bound person. You can keep the cost down or at least spend more money on the right things.

An architect I know designed and built an apartment for his mother in a building he owned that had been a small factory. The second-floor apartment, accessible from the ground floor by an elevator, had a large, tiled bathroom with a double shower, once used by plant employees at the end of their workdays. In that space, he crafted a wheelchair-accessible shower from pieces, including a seat, bought at Home Depot. Removable foam on the floor of the shower leveled the space with the bathroom floor outside. He spent less than $1,000 crafting the shower, after seeing estimates of more than $3,000 for prefab models.

Entry to the building was accomplished by a concrete ramp with a two-tiered railing near the front door. The end of the ramp at the sidewalk could be lowered even farther, for easier wheelchair access. The door to the building opened out, permitting a 90-degree turn so that a wheelchair-bound person entering the building could be assisted. Once inside, the wheelchair-bound person faced the door of a one-stop elevator. For safety's sake, the shaft and elevator doors had two-hour fire ratings, as well as a telephone jack for an emergency phone. To get the elevator to move, the user had to close the gate, which signaled a computerized mechanism that travel was safe. The final cost of the elevator was about $40,000.

A hallway led from the elevator to the door of the apartment. Clearance required to open the door and enter in a wheelchair met or exceeded the 32-inch government standard. Because the doorstop on the bathroom could not be readjusted to a 32-inch clearance, the architect spent $30 each on a pair of offset hinges for the bathroom door that helped him achieve that standard

To create plenty of sources of natural light to help his mother cope with her failing eyesight, he installed large windows and self-flashing skylights from Home Depot. Color is almost as important as light in accessible-housing design. For example, to help his mother find doors to rooms and the apartment itself, he painted them yellow to make them easily distinguishable from the walls.

The kitchen was a design challenge, and an expensive one at that, because all the appliances needed to be accessible from a seated position. A wall oven and separate range added up to $1,000, about three times the cost of a comparable combined version. The single sink became a double one, with the garbage disposal in the smaller side, which opened up the space under the larger sink for accessibility and storage. Because the kitchen was white, different colors of masking tape were used to distinguish cabinets, the stove and oven, and the like. A large storage closet between the kitchen and the space holding the apartment's mechanicals simulated a basement.

In the final analysis, it is all about ingenuity. If you plan carefully and do enough research, ingenuity doesn't have to cost a lot.

38. ALL WORK AND NO PLAY

You don't need to spend a fortune on a home office.

■ ■ ■

Do you really want to take your work home?

We already work harder and longer hours than ever, which kind of makes you wonder why our grandparents went on strike for the eight-hour day. Still, surveys show that home offices are becoming almost standard in new houses, and owners of older homes are carving office space out of bedrooms, attics, and basements. On the other hand, no one can agree on the value a home office adds to your house.

All three of the houses I've owned have had a least one home office, and, since 1985, one or more of those offices have had a computer. So, if I can't talk you into taking it easy, I'm going to try to guide you through the process of locating and building a home office.

The question is, of course, what will you be doing and when, and how isolated do you wish to be? If you will be working when the kids are around, you might want a space far from the maddening crowd. If you brought your work home so you could spend more time with the kids, then you might want to locate the office near where the buffalo roam.

I should mention one thing here. A few years ago, when dot-com was synonymous with success, we believed that everyone would be telecommuting to work someday. But that hasn't happened. Human beings crave contact with other humans, and no matter how bad things get at the office, there's something reassuring about being there, even if you can work from home one or two days a week.

Now, that doesn't apply to people who run businesses from their homes. Those people have a host of different things to consider when locating and building a home office, including accessibility for people with disabilities. No, what we are talking about here is space for telecommuters—or even people who are writing a book.

Maybe what I've done will give you some ideas. At my house, we have three spaces that could qualify under federal tax law as home offices. One, known as the Hobbit Hole, is off the master bedroom and is used by my wife, a television critic, who spends her evenings and weekends watching DVDs and tapes supplied by the networks. The name, inspired by *The Lord of the Rings,* was applied to the space because I have to bow to enter the room from our bedroom. You may read into that what you will. I rarely enter it. Otherwise, I'd spend my life with a phrenologist, having the bumps on my head interpreted.

The location is perfect for my wife's job, because she often reviews programs that might not be appropriate for our 15-year-old, whose bedroom is on the first floor. He has access to the library off the living room, which is equipped with a TV, DVD player, and VCR as well as stereo equipment and lots of books. There's also a television in the sitting room off the kitchen, which has two stuffed chairs and a coffee table, in case he and I can't agree on what to watch.

The Hobbit Hole has essential equipment, such as a big-screen television and DVD and VCR players, which are watched from a custom-made futon. Next to the futon is a halogen lamp that provides plenty of direct light for reading and knitting. Custom-made cupboards store knitting equipment and yarn and provide space for previewed tapes and DVDs.

The house has three telephone lines—two dedicated for computers. One computer line runs from the basement through ductwork to the Hobbit Hole for my wife's computer, on which she writes late reviews for publication and sends them to the office. Her office has a phone/fax machine, too, and both the computer and the phone/fax sit on a large trestle table that provides plenty of workspace.

My home office is in the basement, which, despite being unfinished, is comfortable and cozy and, thanks to a dehumidifier and central air-conditioning, dry and cool. I chose not to finish the space, because I didn't want to go through the permit process and didn't think I needed anything formal. It's clean, the cement block walls have been recently waterproofed and painted, and the floor of the office is covered by rag rugs that have been used in various houses over the years. Photographs and framed posters that we couldn't find room for upstairs hang on the walls to cheer it. Reference books that I need for my work line inexpensive shelves and an étagère.

My office shares a dedicated modem line with the desktop computer in my older son's room, which constitutes the third home office, even though that son is away most of the year at college. My younger son uses it for playing computer games and some schoolwork.

The basement also holds the laundry area, an exercise area, the mechanicals, and lots of shelving for the storage. The office is a rectangular area, about 7 by 10 feet, surrounded by two walls and the basement stairs. My desk was once a kitchen table, so it provides even more work space than my wife's trestle table, holding a laptop, a telephone, and a couple of in/out baskets as well as providing room for miscellaneous storage. There are three low filing cabinets, two holding newspaper tear sheets and one housing household records, because my office is where all the bills are paid. A fluorescent fixture and a desk lamp provide all the lighting.

There's also an old couch that is now covered with book parts. I have a radio tuned to the local classical/jazz station on the desk and an old TV set and VCR sitting on an unused sideboard.

My wife's office cost practically nothing to build, although the TV equipment, the laptop and printer, and the futon are new. My office cost $4.85, for some telephone cable and connectors, if you don't count the paint and the R-13 insulation in the joists above my head. Everything else was sitting around the basement.

Here's the thing: We spend a lot of money on building home offices, to make places that we use for work "pretty." They are workspaces. As long as they do what they were designed to do, they don't have to come out of the pages of *Architectural Digest.* As a matter of fact, I once observed a focus group on home offices that included 25 recent homebuyers. Only one of them could afford to dedicate a room of his house to office space. The rest squeezed a desk and computer into bedrooms, dining rooms, living rooms, and kitchens.

Home offices don't have to be whole rooms. For example, my house has a butler's pantry as you enter the kitchen. It has an outlet and is next to the telephone. Just add a laptop and you have a home office. A home office can be a desk, lamp, and chair in the corner of a bedroom. It can be a computer table at the end of a hallway or in a walk-in closet hidden behind louvered doors.

The bottom line: It doesn't have to be pretty as long as you can work there, which is pretty much what you can say about my work area at the office.

The coffee at home is much better and cheaper, too.

39. HOW LOW CAN YOU FLOW?

Try to hang on to your old toilet as long as you can.

■ ■ ■

I went to flush the toilet in the downstairs bathroom this morning. Nothing happened. Absolutely nothing.

I removed the top of the tank and looked in. Sure enough, the piece of copper connecting the flush handle arm to the flapper had broken after years of use. I was terrified. Could I repair the mechanism? If I couldn't repair it, could the plumber find a replacement mechanism that would let me keep the 3.5 gallon per flush, problem-free toilet. Or would I be forced to replace it with one of those low-flow, 1.6 gallon per flush models?

The reason for my concern: Despite years of testing and frequent announcements that all the bugs have been worked out, 1.6 gallon per flush, low-flow toilets still present problems. Many owners of low-flow toilets say that it takes two or three flushes to get rid of the same waste that a 3.5 gallon per flush older model would wash away in one try.

If you are remodeling a bathroom, you'll have to deal with low-flow toilets, because federal law requires them in residential applications. My advice: If you don't have to replace your current 3.5 gallon toilet, don't. In a recent list of water-saving recommendations, the nonprofit Alliance to Save Energy (http://www.ase.org), in Washington, D.C., purposely left off low-flow toilets. The advocacy group said that focus groups of consumers spent entire sessions complaining about the toilets, and there didn't seem to be much advantage to listing technology that people didn't like alongside front-loading washing machines, which save water and energy at the same time.

Home inspectors, too, hear complaints about low-flow toilets. Because these toilets use half the water of the older models, people try to flush it twice to get it to work. But it doesn't. The toilet will jam and overflow. That's why I highly recommend shut-off valves on toilet supply lines to give you enough time to plunge a plugged-up toilet before water begins pouring through the ceiling below.

A study by the American Water Works Association Research Foundation (http://www.awwarf.org) showed that there are few double-flushers. "Low-flow, 1.6 gallons per flush toilets do not require additional flushes to equal the performance of older, less water-efficient models," the foundation reported. "Individuals living in households with the 1.6 gallons per flush toilets flushed an average of 5.04 times per day. Those living in houses with older, 3.5 gallons per flush toilets flushed an average of 4.92 times per day."

Other consumer surveys reached mixed conclusions. The Metropolitan Water District of Southern California (http://www.mwdh20 .com) asked 1,300 of its customers if they were happy with the performance of their low-flow toilets. These customers received their 13 models of low-flow toilets from 11 manufacturers through rebate programs in 1998 and 1999. People who liked their toilets really liked them, with a satisfaction rating of 8.37 out of 10. Those who didn't like them still gave them a rating of 5.91 out of 10. Most consumers said they had never had a problem with the toilet jamming or blocking. But 67 percent said they had to double-flush at least once a month.

Low-flow plumbing products officially crossed the threshold of the U.S. home in 1992, with the enactment of the Energy Policy and Conservation Act. The act established water-use restrictions for new toilets, showerheads, and faucets. The so-called EPAct set a national manufacturing standard of 1.6 gallons per flush for most toilets beginning January 1, 1994. While acknowledging "anecdotal reports of poor performance of 1.6 gallons per flush toilets," the Environmental Protection Agency says that customer surveys show high satisfaction. "The plumbing industry has steadily made improvements in toilet technology, and market forces should continue to improve overall performance with time," the EPA said.

On the other hand, some people have tried to bring 3.5 gallon toilets over the border from Canada, where they are still manufactured. Other frustrated homeowners have been searching salvage yards, but rarely are they successful. Most salvage operators only pick up high-end old toilets, such as those from mansions that might have been made in Europe in the early part of the last century. The problem with buying those is parts. Some of those parts haven't been made in 60 years, and what do you do if something goes wrong?

The National Association of Home Builders Research Center (http://www.nahbrc.org) in Upper Marlboro, Maryland, tested low-flow toilets that builders had removed from their houses in response to buyer complaints about clogging. Various technologies are used to make a low-flow toilet more functional. Some have large drain passages and redesigned bowls and tanks for easier wash-down. Others supplement the gravity system with water supply line pressure, compressed air, or a vacuum pump.

The research center testing was limited to one-piece or two-piece gravity-flow toilets that could be compared to 3.5 gallon toilets. Some toilets functioned well; others did poorly. Center researchers developed a "clog index." Where each toilet placed on a scale of 1 to 150 was based on how easily the toilet got rid of the sponges and wads of paper that were used in the rigorous testing.

Toilet manufacturers continue to show concern about performance of their products. A lot of research is being conducted into getting more oomph into the flush. If they work properly, low-flow toilets should use a maximum of 1.6 gallons of water per flush, compared with 5 to 7 gallons of water used by a standard toilet. Low-flow toilets alone could save up to 22,000 gallons of water per year for a family of four.

Part of the problem with low-flow toilets is that EPAct wasn't accompanied by any measure of performance for the products that were to be developed, or any provisions to ensure that the new products would perform at least as effectively as their predecessors. "When they started out, the low-end brands performed much better than the big-name brands," said veteran plumber Marcel Paillard, because the big names "didn't make the bowl and flush valve properly to accommodate the lower water use. To get any toilet to flush properly, the water has to reach the water line in the tank, and even though the brand-name models had enough water, the poorly designed bowl and flush valve got in the way.

One manufacturer has developed a low-flow toilet with a gravity-fed, siphon jet system that depends on the downward force of the water from the tank being channeled through strategically placed rim holes. Another low-flow toilet uses pressure rather than gravity to get rid of waste. The toilet has a bellows in the tank, and instead of having the handle on the side, it has a tennis-ball-size gizmo on the lid for flushing. The only problem is that, if you are too curious about how the toilet works and take off the lid to find out, you'll disconnect the flushing device.

Among the highest-scoring low-flow toilets in the research center test were those manufactured by Toto (http://www.totousa.com), a Japanese company with U.S. operations. The key to the successful operation of these low-flow toilets is an increase in siphon power. To achieve this, design features include a 3-inch-diameter flush valve instead of the industry's 2-inch standard. By increasing the diameter, the rate of water flow from tank to bowl is increased. The height of the water in the tank is also increased to achieve higher head pressure. In the bowl's design, the trap way is $2\frac{1}{8}$ inches, allowing easy passage of a 2-inch ball, he said. A water pool at the bottom of the trap way—the so-called "wetted perimeter"—improves flow. The design allows the Toto to reduce turbulence and air pockets that would impede the siphon.

Sometimes, a homeowner unwittingly contributes to a toilet's poor operation. Say you own a low-flow for two years and put chlorine tablets in the tank to help clean the water. The chlorine degrades the flapper, so the homeowner goes to the home center and buys a generic flapper that actually constricts the flow of water from the tank to the bowl. That would require you to flush twice. And you know what good that does. In the Toto's case, however, the only flapper than can be installed is made by Toto.

One new low-flow toilet is more of a curiosity than something you might want to add to your bathroom, but I'm passing along information about it, because it is beginning to appear in new-home design centers. TotoUSA's Neorest integrated toilet has a lid that automatically opens whenever an individual approaches it. When the individual rises, the lid closes automatically, and the unit flushes. The toilet conserves water by flushing at only 1.2 gallons per flush for liquid waste when its sensor is activated by men standing in front of the bowl. Operated by wireless remote, the toilet seat provides a front- and back-aerated warm-water spray that can be regulated for preferred water pressure and temperature. Other features include oscillating spray massage, heated seat, automatic catalytic air deodorizer, and warm air dryer. The Neorest records frequency of use, then reeducates itself weekly. During times when it remembers infrequent use, Neorest goes into sleep mode. You might be thinking the Neorest provides too much information, but the goal is energy efficiency and water conservation.

One curiosity that for 15 minutes was being passed off as a trend needs to be mentioned just as an example of marketing gone awry: urinals in home bathrooms. A few may be finding their way into new homes around the country, but there is no big rush, except in the minds of the urinal manufacturers.

Bidets, maybe. But that is another story.

40. ALL HANDS ON DECK

Everyone has one, so you should, too.

■ ■ ■

A 19th-century architect once remarked that a house without a porch is like a man without an eyebrow. I think the architect's observation can be easily applied to outdoor decks in the 21st century.

Both are designed as transitional spaces between the outdoors and indoors. What this means is that if the deck is off the kitchen, there are fewer steps to the beer in the refrigerator. If your front door opens directly to the living room, the porch is great place to remove wet shoes and coats.

There are about 30 million residential decks in the United States. More than 6.5 million decks are built in the United States annually, at a total cost of $1.9 billion to $3 billion. The average life expectancy of a deck is 11 years. About once a decade, a homeowner upgrades, expands, or replaces their deck.

Until recently, most new-home buyers opted for decks over front porches. In the last 15 years or so, there has been some movement back to porches, thanks to what is known alternately as neotraditionalism or New Urbanism among architects. Neotraditionalism sees greater value in the way we built houses before 1950 than since. One of the values of a front porch is that it encourages interaction among neighbors.

When I was growing up in a city neighborhood in the early 1950s, porches functioned as social centers. The problem with porches, especially on older houses, is that they need to be maintained, and that can be expensive. More importantly, and despite the merits of the neotraditionalist argument, being out front exposes us not only to neighbors but to street noises and the prying eyes of strangers. The result is that there's a whole lot of decking going on on the back side of the house.

My own deck building experience left me with mixed feelings. The deck was designed to replace a collapsing back porch, but it didn't free me from having to spend hundreds of dollars repairing a wraparound front porch that had been neglected for years. The deck was a beautiful piece of work, a bi-level structure of about 260 square feet onto which the kitchen door opened. It overlooked the backyard and was surrounded by gardens. The top level had a roof. It cost $5,000 in 1987 dollars.

We rarely used it. The summer sun shone directly on it from about 11 AM on, and by early evening, the heat was brutal. Surrounded as it was by gardens, the deck was buggy. I made the mistake of planting grapes in an adjacent garden, and the yellow jackets attracted by the fruit swarmed the deck in September and October.

The deck was also maintenance-intensive, owing to its location on the north side of the house. I'd spend a week every six months cleaning and resealing the wood simply to keep up with it. That's only if there was a rain-free period that would allow two coats of sealer to dry. Once, thanks to a warm spell in early December, I was able apply the second coat of sealer to the deck by the light of a full moon at 5 AM, before I left for work

There is a positive side to this story. It is the one you need to focus on. My deck proved its value when we sold our house. This doesn't mean that I recovered everything I spent on it over 14 years in any recognizable fashion. The buyers competing for our house didn't say, "And here's $6,000 for the deck," but the deck was a selling tool. If we didn't have one, we wouldn't have been able to compete in our real estate market.

If you have room for a patio made of brick or interlocking concrete pavers, consider putting one in. Patios are becoming popular gathering places for entertaining. Except for occasional weeding between the pavers, they tend to involve less maintenance than the typical wooden deck, although deck builders are now using composite lumber decking and vinyl railings and posts that reduce the amount of cleaning.

When weighing your choices, you'll need to consider whether a deck or a patio is more in keeping with the style of your house. If you have a Colonial-style house and add a wooden deck, it probably will not attract positive comment. Still, decks appear to be the overwhelming choice of homeowners.

You'll need to think about many factors when considering a deck. One of the most important considerations is the kind of lumber you want to use. Wood treated with chromated copper arsenic (CCA), the pesticide long used as a preservative, has been phased out of residential use. Treated-lumber producers are beginning to offer less-suspect alternatives to CCA that are more costly, at least initially.

Arsenic is a known human carcinogen, and the government believes that any reduction in the levels of potential exposure is desirable. However, the new lumber, in addition to being pricier than the banned variety, comes with its own problems. The new treatments, alkaline copper quaternary (ACQ) or copper azole (CA), contain a higher level of copper than CCA, which means that they corrode fasteners and fittings used in deck construction twice as rapidly as the banned preservative. Aluminum or electroplated fasteners and fittings that worked perfectly with CCA lumber can be a disaster if used with the new lumber.

Brian Sakal, a building official in Upper Merion Township, Pennsylvania, has had to order a number of decks using the new lumber to be rebuilt, because the wrong fasteners and fittings were used. He said that only hot-dipped, galvanized and stainless steel fasteners are acceptable for use with ACQ and CA treated lumber, but contractors and do-it-yourselfers appear to be unaware of that fact. "It's good when we can catch the error before it becomes a problem that can cause a deck to collapse, resulting in injury and even death," Sakal says. "Of course, it costs the builder and the homeowner time and money to make the changes, especially if the deck has been completed, but what I and other officials fear is that there are a lot of decks being built without permits, especially by do-it-yourselfers, that may fly under our radar screen."

Do you need to replace the old CCA-treated lumber, which has been linked to health problems in children? Not at all. You'll need to take precautions, however, such as washing your hands after handling the material and not permitting children to play in soil that comes in contact with the wood.

Other kinds of wood are naturally resistant to rot and insects, but they also are more expensive. One of the chief advantages of the CCA-treated Southern pine two-by-four was cost. Western red cedar, naturally resistant except where it comes into contact with the ground, has been running almost five times the cost of CCA lumber. However, Western red cedar, which comes primarily from coastal forests in the Northwest, is a beautiful alternative that doesn't chip and crack like pressure-treated yellow pine.

Engineered or composite lumber is making headway as decking, although no one has yet found a way to use it in structural applica-

tions. In combination with pressure-treated redwood or cedar framing, however, it is a maintenance-free though somewhat expensive
alternative. The best advice is to shop around.

Before you build a deck, you've got to have a plan. You can work
one out with your deck builder or look around for a deck you like, put
the specs down on paper, and then tailor the specs to fit your situation.

Decks don't always have to be part of the house, even though it's
usually more convenient to have them near the kitchen. A freestand-
ing deck in the yard often provides more design flexibility than is
offered by stacking it alongside the house. In fact, for the greatest financial return, many builders and real estate agents suggest that the
deck be designed as an extension of the living space, not an appendage to the house. Most people also tend to build their decks too
small for furniture and function. Add a couple more feet than you
think you'll need. Every inch will be used.

I've emphasized much of this before, but it never hurts to say it
more than once: Every municipality has its own requirements for
decks and their builders. In some, builders must be licensed; most are
required to be insured. Other towns and cities require that a scale
drawing of the deck plan be reviewed by the building inspector. The
contractor handles all permit and inspection requirements and builds
their cost into the price. Many provide the required scale drawings
once the contract has been signed.

When I had my deck built, I looked around at decks at other
houses and talked to homeowners, contractors, and building officials
to get a general idea of what the process entails. What follows is a
brief list of the basics of deck building, so you can keep an eye on
construction:

- Post holes are dug with a shovel or post-hole digger according to the specifications established by the local building department, which will inspect them after they are done.
- Concrete is then poured for the footings, 450 to 500 pounds
  for each hole. Footings can be built on 24 hours after they've
  been poured.

- A heavy "ledger board," typically a 2-by-12, is attached to the house with galvanized bolts or 40d nails. Joists will be attached to the ledger board using metal joist hangers.
- Four-by-four or six-by-six posts that support the deck are anchored to the footings. The two-by-ten joists are attached from the ledger board to a crossbeam that has been attached to the posts. While most contractors use metal joist hangers, some bolt the crossbeam to the posts so that the weight rests on the bolts.
- The flooring and four-by-four rail posts are attached. On a wide deck, decking boards of varying lengths are used instead of a single length, to avoid having a seam down the middle.
- Railings are built in sections by attaching two-by-two balusters a few inches apart to two-by-four precut cross rails, so that the balusters will be on the inside rather than the outside of the deck—they look better that way. The railings are attached to the rail posts, which are notched to accept the railings flush. Then the rail posts are cut to make them even with the railings. The railings are capped, often with a fairly wide board, often a five/four-by-six.
- Stairs are built and options added. Options may include benches and latticework.

It sounds simple, and unless something needs to be demolished to make space for the deck, as was my experience, fairly straightforward.

The bottom line: Make it pretty. Make sure it is functional and safe. Clean and seal it regularly. But most of all, try to use it as much as you can.

41. A TANKLESS JOB

You can have all the hot water you want, when you want it.

■ ■ ■

Tankless water heaters are designed to provide hot water immediately just by turning the faucet.

If you are thinking about renovating a kitchen or bathroom, interested in heating water at point of use in a vacation house, or looking for an alternative to your aging storage-type gas or electric water heater, you might consider one of the growing number of tankless water heaters on the market.

A tankless water heater is designed to provide hot water instantly by turning on a faucet. Some plumbers argue against them, in spite of the improvements, saying the heater coils are prone to rusting. Still, the heaters are becoming the talk of the housing industry, even though they've been available in the United States for several years.

Tankless, or demand, heaters also made the list of top ten technologies chosen by the Partnership for Advancing Technology in Housing (http://www.toolbase.org), a public-private initiative administered by the Department of Housing and Urban Development (http://www.hud.gov). Take it from someone who looks at a few hundred home-related products that debut annually: it usually takes any new technology quite a while—typically 15 years—to go from the drawing board to widespread use. Tankless heaters have taken about five years.

It is easy to see why. Tankless units heat and deliver water on demand. Cold water is circulated through a series of burners or electric coils that heat the water as it passes through. Tankless units cost more than storage heaters, but because you are not heating a big tank of water 24 hours a day, they cost less to operate.

Not surprisingly, having abundant hot water is important to homeowners. A nationwide survey of 800 homeowners by Public Opinion

Strategies of Washington, D.C., found that 90 percent of respondents considered hot water the one convenience they could not do without. By comparison, 52 percent said they could live without a TV. Heating water accounts for 20 percent or more of a typical household's annual energy expenditures, according to the Department of Energy. The yearly operating cost for conventional storage-tank water heaters averages $200 for gas units or $450 for electric ones.

Storage-tank water heaters raise the water temperature to the setting on the tank, usually between 120 and 140 degrees, and maintain it there. Even if no hot water is drawn from the tank (and cold water enters the tank), the heater will operate periodically to maintain the temperature. This is the result of what are called "standby losses," the heat conducted and radiated from the walls of the tank and, in gas-fired water heaters, through the flue pipe. Standby losses represent 10 to 20 percent of a household's annual water heating costs.

Although tankless heaters have been popular in Europe and Japan for a long time—indeed, several manufacturers of units available in this country are Japanese—concern over having enough hot water has kept them on the back burner, so to speak. Even the largest, whole-house tankless gas models cannot supply enough hot water for simultaneous multiple uses, such as showers and laundry, according to the Energy Department. Large users of hot water, such as clothes washers and dishwashers, need to be operated separately.

On the other hand, separate demand, or point-of-use, electric tankless heaters can be installed underneath sinks or in closets near the shower, sink, or washer to handle individual hot-water loads. Point-of-use heaters for sinks and showers have long been popular with owners of vacation houses with electric service. Unlike tankless gas heaters, the electric ones do not require outside venting. They also are much smaller than tank heaters. Although sizes vary, the average is about 24 inches high, 18 inches wide, and 9 inches deep—taking up a little more than 2 cubic feet. Tankless units are wall-mounted and can be placed indoors or outdoors.

In a demonstration house built at the annual International Builders Show in Las Vegas in January 2004, a tankless unit that supplied hot water to the 5,300-square-foot residence took up 16 square feet less than the comparable tank heater.

Some the largest residential gas units manufactured by Rinnai can supply 8.5 gallons per minute. A compact model manufactured by Takagi Industrial Company USA provides 240 gallons of hot water per hour and takes up only 2.2 cubic feet of space. A 7.4 gallon per minute model that Rheem Manufacturing Company makes is more a whole-house tankless than a point-of-use unit. The heater needs to be properly sized for the house. If you don't have the right size of heater, you'll run out of water in the middle of a shower if someone decides to wash dishes in the kitchen sink.

Electric tankless models are not designed for whole-house operation. Most residential gas-fired models now on the market typically supply only 5 gallons of water per minute heated by 90 degrees. Electrically heated models provide even less hot water: 2 gallons a minute heated by 70 degrees. By providing hot water immediately where it is used, tankless heaters waste less water: people do not need to let the water run as they wait for warmer water to reach a remote faucet.

Equipment life may be longer than for tank-type heaters, because tankless models are less subject to corrosion, despite what some plumbers will tell you. The expected life of tankless water heaters is 20 years, compared with 10 to 15 years for tank-type heaters.

Tankless heaters range in price from $200 for a small under-sink unit to $1,000 for a gas-fired unit that delivers five gallons per minute. Those numbers do not include installation, which can add $150 to $300 to the price. Typically, the more hot water a unit produces, the higher the cost. Electric tankless heaters typically cost more to operate than gas units.

There are some drawbacks to demand water heating, and you and your contractor need to be aware of them before you decide that your project must go tankless. Unless your demand system has a feature called *modulating temperature control,* it may not heat water to a constant temperature at different flow rates. That means that water temperatures can fluctuate uncomfortably—particularly if the pressure varies wildly in your water system.

Electric tankless units will draw more instantaneous power than tank-type water heaters. If electric rates include a demand charge, operation may be expensive. Electric units also require a relatively high power draw, because water must be heated quickly to the desired temperature. Make sure your wiring is up to the demand.

Tankless gas water heaters require a direct vent or conventional flue. If a gas-powered unit has a pilot light, it can waste a lot of energy, and, depending on design and the cost of gas, pilot lights can cost $12 to $20 per year to operate. Many of the newer gas-fired units take that into consideration by not having pilot lights.

42. DON'T FEEL INSECURE

A security system protects your investment and saves money.

■ ■ ■

Since the terrorist attacks on the World Trade Center and the Pentagon on 9/11, home security firms nationwide have been reporting a surge in interest in alarm systems. Although it is highly unlikely that individual homes will be invaded by terrorists, and no burglar alarm could prevent what the government couldn't, interest in residential security systems tends to increase in times of economic downturns, when break-ins and thefts tend to rise.

During the booming 1990s, lower crime rates helped draw more people downtown in New York, Chicago, Philadelphia, and other cities. Because real estate sales have not slowed in most places, the downtown trend continues. But unlike in the 1990s, more city homebuyers these days are looking into alarm systems.

Among suburban buyers, whether to install security seems to depend on the price range of the house. At the higher end, optional security systems are usually purchased. At the lower end, the answer is no.

In both new and older houses, prices of security systems can range from a few hundred to several thousand dollars. Although state-of-the-art systems can be costly, many homeowners are willing to pay the price, even if the expense is not justified by crime statistics. Whether you spend money on a burglar alarm system or just make a few changes to make your house more secure, the money you spend may pay you back with a feeling of security.

According to federal crime data, 38 percent of assaults occur during a burglary. Houses on corner lots are more likely to be burglarized. If your home has had a burglary, the odds of it being burglarized again increase dramatically, because burglars correctly assume that the items they appropriated have been replaced with new items.

Fear of murder and mayhem, whether real or imagined, is often strong enough to overcome concerns about cost, maintenance, or monitoring fees. Some crime-prevention experts believe that by simply altering one's surroundings, a homeowner or a neighborhood can reduce crime. Such remedies can be as simple as cutting overgrown foliage away from the front of a house or as complex as rearranging streetlights to reduce shadows in which criminals can lurk.

The basic philosophy centers on the commonsense use of the physical environment to reduce the opportunities for crime. The three main strategies are using physical design elements such as fences and street closures to limit access to an area to those who live there; using windows, lighting, and landscaping to help homeowners see intruders as well as keep an eye on their neighbors' houses; and making public property easily distinguishable from private property, using landscaping and porches. Some house designs, while charming and attractive, can encourage criminal activity. Recessed doorways and alcoves can become hiding places. Walls and fences with crosspieces can be used as ladder rungs.

The insurance industry provides a major incentive for installing home security equipment. Companies that underwrite homeowners policies usually offer a discount of up to 20 percent on annual premiums for houses with security systems, according to the Insurance Information Institute in New York. The size of the discount is typically determined by the sophistication of the equipment, regardless of whether it is connected to a central monitoring system at the burglar alarm company, and the distance from the house to the nearest police or fire station. The reason for such discounts is obvious. In the next 20 years, three out of four homes in the United States will be burglarized, according to FBI statistics. The average property loss in a burglary exceeds $1,000, not to mention the damage from entry.

From all available evidence, reliable home security should be a blend of technology and common sense. For example, a barking canine inside a house can make a burglar think twice about breaking in.

Before determining the precautions you should take and the equipment you should buy, you should know something about burglars. There are three types: the professional, the semiprofessional, and the amateur. Most homeowners, according to the Burglary Prevention Council in Chicago, have to be concerned with the latter two.

Residential burglars often are teenage boys who live near your home. They are opportunists looking for easy targets. If the risk of detection is too high, the typical amateur burglar will not attempt to enter your home. Both amateurs and semiprofessionals will spend a few hours to a week scouting the neighborhood and its homes. After determining the target, a typical amateur burglar spends only a few minutes burglarizing it.

When your house is unoccupied—whether for a few minutes or a few weeks—it is vulnerable. Keep that in mind when determining the precautions you'll need to take to increase security, or call in a professional to do it.

43.   WILL IT WASH?

Put the laundry room anywhere but the basement.

■ ■ ■

It's probably just a marketing tool to sell more washing machines, but one major manufacturer, Whirlpool, has been pushing the concept of what I call the "super laundry room."

The correct name is the Whirlpool® Family Studio, and it's not only for washing and drying clothes. The space is designed to accommodate all the messy chores, crafts, sewing, homework, and gardening projects. If you don't want to look at it, you simply close the door. Including a variety of newfangled laundry-related tools, cabinets, counters, and workspaces, the cost is about $30,000. In a new house, you can add that to the mortgage and pay for it over a few hundred months. In older houses—well, a midrange kitchen addition costs about that much, and you might able to work a modest but workable laundry area into a corner of it.

Getting back to reality, here are a few things you should know about laundry and trends before you decide where you want a new and improved one.

A builders' association survey found that 92 percent of buyers wanted a laundry room among a home's extra rooms for convenience and luxury. Where to put that laundry room did not have such a clear-cut answer. The survey showed that 26 percent wanted it near the bedrooms, 26 percent near the kitchen, 23 percent in the basement, and 10 percent in the garage.

Another study showed that having a laundry room in the basement tended to detract from a house's sale price. Yet owners of existing houses often have no choice but to put the laundry room in the basement: Apart from having the needed space, it often is the place with ready access to hot water and drainage, and it has somewhere unobtrusive to vent the dryer.

Why do we need to think about laundry at all? One manufacturer's survey found that 20 million women and 8 million men do laundry each day, and that the typical family does eight to ten loads per week. When Maytag test-marketed its Neptune® washer in Bern, Iowa, a few years back, it found that the average Bern family (two adults and two children) did 11 loads a week. According to the manufacturers, a load of clothes takes more than two hours from start to finish, including collecting them, transporting them, sorting them, washing them, drying them, returning them to bedrooms, and putting them away. With those numbers—two hours per load, eight to ten loads per week—having the washer and dryer close to where the clothing is dropped off and picked up takes on greater significance.

Location is best determined by the age and needs of the home-owner. If you have younger children, you will be doing a lot of laundry. Because there is so much of it, you'll want to locate the washer and dryer where you can keep an eye on the children. A finished basement with a play area is ideal, and this is probably not what the two professors meant about the negative effect of a basement laundry on sale price. If you don't have a finished basement, a spot near the kitchen is also ideal, especially if the kitchen opens onto a family room so that the children always will be in view.

If you have teenagers or are older and don't want to have to carry laundry for long distances, a second-floor laundry room is what you need. If you don't have lots of space, a stacked washer and dryer fit into a closet.

No matter where you locate the laundry, you'll need to consider a number of things to make the room efficient and cost-effective. An area six feet wide by three feet deep would accommodate a standard-size washer and dryer, a utility tub, and maybe a hamper. (A stackable washer/dryer unit could save space horizontally.) A 7½-foot or 8-foot ceiling would provide more than enough height for a couple of shelves to hold supplies and detergent above the washer and dryer.

But is that enough room to meet your needs? Not necessarily. You might want additional space for sorting dirty laundry and folding clean clothes. Maybe even for an ironing board. Try to place the laundry room near existing plumbing and wiring, preferably in the rear of the house, so that the vent is unobtrusive. Building codes require flexible ductwork for the dryer vent and shut-off valves for the water.

If the room is on the other side of the master bath, you'll need to insulate to deaden the sound. You may need to bring in a structural engineer to see whether your floor joists can withstand a washer's vibration. If not, the floor will need reinforcing. You'll need six inches of clearance behind the dryer for the venting duct and gas connections (if you're using gas). Most dryers are 30 to 32 inches deep.

Building codes also require that the washer sit in an overflow pan to prevent water from pouring onto the floor and into the ceiling below.

Doors can be solid or louvered, but with solid ones you will need a mechanical way (a vent with a fan) to bring enough air into the space for proper combustion for a gas dryer. This is not an issue with an electric dryer. There should be three feet of clearance for the door, so the washer and dryer can be moved in and out of the laundry room easily.

Plan for plenty of lighting. Ground fault circuit interrupter outlets will shut off automatically if they come into contact with moisture. You may want to replace existing drywall with what is known as green board for moisture control. But a vent fan can achieve the same effect.

44. OH, DRY UP!

No basement is completely free of moisture.

■ ■ ■

There is no such thing as a completely dry basement.

This doesn't mean that you have to spend your days waiting for the cellar to fill with water. It simply means that the basement, more than any other area of the house, is affected by moisture, and you have to consider the most efficient way to control any dampness before you spend thousands of dollars turning the space into what may turn out to be an indoor swimming pool.

For example, air-conditioning ductwork in basements "sweats" when cold metal comes into contact with damper air. Rather than having water dripping from the ducts onto the rug, a dehumidifier properly sized for the space will keep the basement drier. Of course, you'll need to find the proper humidity setting and empty the dehumidifier bucket when it's full, but that's the price you pay for a drier basement. The size you buy is based on water removal from a certain number of square feet over 24 hours.

If water gets into the basement during heavy rains, you might solve the problem by cleaning gutters so the water will not be diverted to portions of the foundation that are more susceptible to leaks. You also should be certain that areas around the foundation are graded properly. When rain falls, it should be flowing away from the foundation, not toward it. A possible solution is to regrade, first banking soil against the foundation to achieve a minimum grade of 2 percent, which most engineers consider enough to divert water away from the foundation.

More chronic basement problems often require exterior excavation, especially when water flows from the point where the floor meets the wall. A drainage field is created along the perimeter, and a waterproofing agent is used.

Most companies that handle leaky basements try to do it from the inside—for example, by installing a subfloor drainage system. The system does not get rid of the water problem; it just manages it. Drainage is installed to direct the water to a place where it will not do any damage, usually to a sump, where, when the water reaches a certain level, it is pumped through a PVC drain line, typically placed above ground away from the house.

If you have a pump, make sure it works. If there is no water in the sump, add enough water to trigger the pump mechanism that otherwise operates automatically. Sounds simple, doesn't it? It isn't all that simple. A lot of municipalities won't let you pump the water from the sump into the soil line, which is below the frost line and thus protected from the cold. What some people do is install a diverter that will let the sump pump send water through the soil line in the winter and through the above-ground drain line in warm weather.

That's illegal, of course. Even if it weren't, the homeowner would need to install a device that prevents sewage from the soil line flowing back into the sump. A better solution would be a dry well somewhere in the yard to handle the water from the sump without turning the lawn above into a swamp. The water flowing into the dry well should percolate harmlessly into the ground. That way, the drain line from the sump pump can be buried below the frost line so it can work properly even in the deepest freezes.

Why is the basement such a big deal anyway?

It's a perfect site for storage. We've acquired so much stuff, we need every bit of space we have to keep it. Expansion is another reason, which makes basements one of the top locations for renovation. It's the stuff of which extra bedrooms and family rooms are made in both older and newer houses.

Having a basement to convert to living space makes a house sell faster and for more money. Growing families with limited funds usually can add a basement bedroom for much less than buying a new house. But then there's the moisture issue. The growing demand for basement living space has led to a proliferation of basement waterproofing systems and companies. Some know what they are doing. Some haven't a clue.

One homeowner spent $7,600 on a basement waterproofing system that included a back-up battery for the sump pump in the event of a power failure. When even the battery backup failed and his basement filled with water, the damage was $2,700, with all but the deductible paid by the insurer. The homeowner believed the waterproofing company's guarantee would pay the difference. But a careful reading of the contract discovered that "consequential or incidental" damages weren't covered.

Guess what kind of damage this was?

Even with the system working, the next heavy rain raised the water table enough to permeate the basement floor. A month after the homeowner called the company for help, a representative showed up. The solution: a second sump and a second pump, both at the homeowner's expense.

Even when they have a clue, some contractors don't get it completely. Alen Malott hired a company to install a drainage system around the perimeter of his basement. "The guy first said he was going to use a jackhammer to cut the concrete for the drains but then decided to use a wet saw," Malott said. "In both cases, the workman should have wet down the area to reduce the amount of dust kicked up by the work. He didn't. When the furnace came on, it sucked up the dust floating in the basement air. The furnace blower fan carried the dust to every room in the house. It's been three years, and I'm still finding dust."

45. AN IDEA THAT DOESN'T ALWAYS HOLD WATER

Swimming pools may please you, but they rarely add value.

■ ■ ■

Jack Severson had a spacious backyard that could easily accommodate a large swimming pool, which would provide plenty of entertainment for his children and grandchildren in the summer and daily exercise for him and his wife.

He assumed it would be an easy task to have one built. Instead, he ended up in court. On the first day of construction, the pool contractor hit ground water at a depth of four feet. After a few days of deciding what to do, digging resumed, a pump was installed, and after a week, it was clear that the pump would do the job of keeping the excavation dry and construction would continue.

Except that it didn't. Over the course of five months, construction proceeded fitfully. A team of specialists would show up, do its part (installing reinforcing rods for the concrete, for example), and then no one would come to do the second phase for weeks on end. The contractor did not return phone calls—ever—until Jack filed suit. Within five weeks, the job was virtually completed.

Things happen, of course, and we can't usually predict what is beneath the ground until we hit it. An experienced pool contractor, however, should be more than aware of the potential problems and be prepared to handle them. Jack's problem was that he couldn't get the contractor to commit to anything, including a completion date or returning phone calls. Jack took his first swim on Labor Day weekend. The pool work had started in early March, and Jack expected to be in the swim by Memorial Day. Is he pursuing his lawsuit even though his pool has been completed? You bet he is.

At least Jack was building a pool for the right reason: to enjoy it. Too often, homeowners spend $25,000 or more on an in-ground pool hoping to add value to the house. That's when it ends up being a liability, because not everyone wants a house with a pool.

In California, Florida, southern Texas, and the desert Southwest, houses without swimming pools do tend to sell for less or spend more time on the market without buyers. Having one does not add value to a house as much as not having one takes away from it. But that makes perfect sense, because pools are used almost year-round in warmer parts of the country, meaning that having to maintain them is cost-effective.

The same cannot be said around the rest of the country, however. New-home builders in colder climates have long recognized that some people are swimmers and others aren't, so they tend to build large pools attached to clubhouses stocked with other forms of exercise. In fact, a few years back, a homebuilder in the Middle Atlantic region offered buyers either a full-size swimming pool or $15,000 worth of upgrades. Less than half chose to have their own pool.

A pool can add an average of $20,000 to $40,000 to the cost of a new home, although lower interest rates over the last few years have reduced the expense by spreading payments for the pool over the length of a mortgage. If you already own a house and plan to borrow to pay for a pool, that's another story.

Appraisers tell me that people are always asking them if it would it be worth it to put in a pool. The standard answer: If you spent $100,000 to do it, you might recover $25,000 on your investment when you sell the house. The question that follows is why the homeowner wants the pool at all. If the homeowner will have guests all the time using the pool, the homeowner will have to foot a large bill for upkeep and care. Pool maintenance costs can be high even when the pool is not in use, especially if a maintenance service is under contract to take care of it regularly.

On the other hand, some homeowners initially opposed to having a pool warm up to pools after living with them for a time.

Several years ago, Lance Parry was shopping for a house, and found one he liked that had a pool. "We didn't want a pool, so we passed on the house at first," he said. "But we couldn't find a house we liked as much, so we bought the place with the pool."

As it turned out, his children used the pool extensively during what is a four-month season, in good years, and became excellent swimmers. In addition, pool parties kept the children and their friends under the parents' watchful eyes. The pool was such a good fit for Parry and his family, in fact, that he eventually spent almost $20,000 rebuilding the deck and upgrading the pool.

The interest in pools appears to be highest among people with no children or families with teenagers, real estate agents and builders say. People with small children are the least likely to want a house with a pool. They have nightmares about the children getting up in the middle of the night and drowning. Those concerns are justified. A child can drown in less than five minutes, in only two inches of water. About 350 children under 5 drown in pools each year. And 2,600 children are treated in hospital emergency rooms each year for near-drowning incidents—the vast majority of which happen in backyard pools.

Jim Remsen bought a house with a pool but ended up having it dug up and filled in. His children were small, and the pool was a potential hazard to both his own children and those of his neighbors. "It was more trouble than it was worth," he said. Removing it, however, opened up much of the yard for a play area that the children could use all year, as well as a garden for Remsen.

Safety experts recommend that fences and walls at least four feet high be installed completely around a pool. Fence gates should be self-closing and self-latching. The latch should be out of a small child's reach. That's not only a safety requirement. Such security precautions need to be taken before a homeowners insurance company will even consider providing additional coverage. Be aware that it is additional coverage, not part of your standard homeowners policy, and thus will raise your annual premium.

"Swimming pools are everyone's dream but not everyone's reality, said Realtor Noelle Barbone, who has owned three houses with pools. "A swimming pool will draw people" to a house for sale, she said, "but when they work out the numbers—heater, filters, opening and closing the pool for a relatively brief season—second thoughts usually win out."

46. NOT JUST A HOLE IN THE WALL

Efficient windows save money and energy.
Just be sure they fit the house.

■ ■ ■

Although there are no guarantees that the money you spend on replacement windows will be recouped when you sell your house, there are several good reasons to do it anyway. The choice is either to refurbish the existing windows to make them work as they were designed or to replace them with more energy-efficient models.

If your house has a few windows, replacing them might not be a budget breaker. However, if you live in a house with 25 or more windows of various sizes, expect money to be tight for a while. A recent estimate for replacing five double-hung, wood windows with new wood windows came to $2,500, or $500 per window, including labor.

One problem with replacing windows in older houses is that they are often odd-sized. Before World War II, there was no universal construction standard, so builders made windows in sizes unique to that house. Replacing the old windows often requires expensive customization. In addition, when replacing a window, you have to consider how the new window fits the overall appearance of the house.

Sometimes, the decision to replace windows in an older house doesn't rest solely with the homeowner. Historic districts have rules governing replacement windows. Whatever changes you make to the exterior of your house are governed by those rules, and even if the windows you want are more efficient than what you have now, you have to comply with what the historic commission wants.

In new construction, standard windows are not that expensive compared with the total cost of the house. Special windows—transoms, half-moons, and Palladian—add a considerable amount to the cost, however. Windows in new houses, in fact, can approach 3 percent of the sale price. For a $300,000, 3,200-square-foot house, that means $9,000. Divide that by 25 standard windows, and you are talking $360 a window. Vinyl windows, which are common in new construction, are less expensive than wood ones, with a price difference of about $60. Price should never be the sole deciding factor, though.

A lot of people who want replacement windows really don't know what the windows are supposed to do, or they aren't really up on the latest advances in energy efficiency. Efficient windows are much more widely available than they were a decade ago, thanks to the rapid growth of new technologies. In the postwar years, replacement windows were aluminum. Aluminum was a conductor of cold temperatures, however, so in the mid-1960s, a West German scientist developed vinyl windows, and they were introduced in the United States in the 1970s. Because many homebuyers and homeowners don't like the look of vinyl, no matter how maintenance-free it is, manufacturers and builders began offering wooden windows or ones that had vinyl on the outside and wood inside.

When buying a new or old house, how do you tell whether the windows are sound or will need to be replaced? Having owned two older houses with older windows—one of them had 31 to be exact—I have been able to turn window inspection into both science and an art form.

First, you need to look at each window in the house to see whether it operates as it was designed. Sometimes windows in new construction have been installed too tightly, so they pinch the screens, which won't open and close easily. In older houses, you usually find that the top sash has been painted shut because people rarely move it up and down.

Windows in very old or historic houses usually operate surprisingly well. A lot of old-house owners like living in those houses because they have history attached to them, and they have maintained the windows so as not to detract from the look. In fact, purists among old-house owners often don't care about efficiency. Having leaky windows is a part of owning an old house. You can make them more efficient, but replacing them rarely comes up.

To make my older windows more efficient, I stripped and painted each sash, replaced the glass and hardware, and installed new weights and chains so that they move up and down easily. To compensate for their inefficiency, I sealed the gaps between the moving parts with weather stripping or filled the gaps between the window frame and the wall with caulk. Although I installed storm windows to reduce heat loss, there are temporary fixes, such as plastic film kits that create the effect of an interior storm window at lower cost than an exterior one.

My newest house, although built in 1929, has energy-efficient windows, which were installed by the previous owners at about $400 each. They have brought me a level of comfort unknown in my historically correct but very airy previous homes. The nonprofit Alliance to Save Energy (http://www.ase.org) in Washington, D.C., maintains that replacing windows adds value to a house in several ways. It improves the appearance and resale value of the home. It reduces maintenance costs such as painting and makes cleaning easier with tilt-sash designs. It improves comfort by making windows feel warmer in the winter and by cutting down unwanted solar heat in summer, and it reduces damage to furnishings by blocking ultraviolet light that can damage fabrics and other materials.

The kind of replacement windows you buy is determined by the kind of house you own. They can actually detract from the value if they aren't appropriate for the architectural style. If you are planning to sell a house and are installing low-end, $99 replacement windows to spruce the place up, then the replacement qualifies as maintenance, and the return won't be very high. But if you are planning to stay and are replacing your old windows with high-end new ones, you are remodeling and will recoup much of the costs.

The biggest test of the energy efficiency of a replacement window is the gas, electric, or oil bill for the following year. Double-pane windows with a low-e—emissivity—coating can reduce heating bills by 34 percent in cold climates, compared with uncoated, single-pane windows, according to Alliance to Save Energy.

What energy-efficient features should your replacement windows have? According to the Efficient Windows Collaborative (http://www .efficientwindows.org), a group of insulation and window manufacturers that comply with federal energy requirements, new windows should have low-e coatings, which let in visible light but block radiant heat losses to cut heating bills. They should have solar control, or spectrally-selective, coatings to block solar heat gain to save cooling energy but let in visible light. The windows should have insulated frames. Metal frames without insulation are the least efficient. Vinyl, insulated vinyl, fiberglass, and wood frames are more efficient.

The invisible gas filler in a double-pane window is critical to energy efficiency. Instead of plain air, high-efficiency models use argon or krypton gas, which conducts very little heat and helps the window's insulating properties. The material used to create the separation between the two panes of glass, called a thermal break, was traditionally metal. New materials insulate better and make the overall window more efficient. In a warm climate, retrofit films can be applied to windows to reduce solar gain and cut cooling costs.

47. SMOKE GETS IN YOUR EYES

Everyone wants a fireplace, as long as little work is involved.

■ ■ ■

Nothing says *romantic* like a fireplace. Yet nothing offers an opportunity for a lot of work than a wood-burning one, such as storing wood in a way that won't attract bugs and termites, and hauling in wood in the depths of winter, trying to keep your balance on the ice, as well as getting rid of the ash without getting it all over the house.

Then there's the expense of paying someone to clean the creosote from the chimney. A bird will build its nest in the flue, and when you light the fire, smoke finds its way back into the living room, stinging your eyes, making you cough, and triggering the smoke and carbon-monoxide alarms.

That's not so romantic.

So why do you put up with a wood-burning fireplace when it costs about $1,100, including installation, to have a gas insert installed in the hearth? The new ones come with carbon-monoxide detectors and air-depletion sensors to reduce the danger of asphyxiation. They also replicate the look of burning wood, without the crackle, and require nothing more than remembering to turn off the pilot light before you go to bed or leave the house.

Whether it is used regularly or just sits idly in the living room looking pretty, a fireplace is one of the things that seems to make a house a home. Real estate listing agents say that whether or not they use the fireplaces, buyers want to see them. They provide a focal point in the house and have decorative value. Some people may simply put plants in them, but even so, they provide that sense of warmth—hearth and home. And hearth and home seem to have become more important since the events of 9/11 made us look at our houses as refuges and retreats rather than simply shelters.

In suburban and rural areas, fireplaces take on added duties, providing an alternative source of heat and light during winter storms. Even in normally warm areas, fireplaces are a standard feature. In California, you cannot sell a house without a fireplace, even though you probably don't need one more than three days a year. Fireplaces are part of what is known as *lifestyle,* or spending money on things you don't really need.

Fireplaces have been around forever as a source of heat and a place to cook, but their importance to the homeowner declined precipitously with the advent of the cook stove and central heating in the late 19th century. Many houses built between 1900 and 1950 didn't have fireplaces, and many homeowners closed up their hearths or buried them behind walls rather than deal with maintenance and fire code issues. If you are opening the walls for a project anyway, you might consider adding a fireplace or renewing an existing one.

In the last few years, the concept of fireplaces has changed. The shift from masonry to prefab designer boxes has put fireplaces in bathrooms, dining rooms, and bedrooms as well as living rooms and family rooms. Fireplaces can be seen in the walls of entertainment rooms, below big-screen televisions, so that you have your choice of what you want to see.

The increase in locations results from advances in technology: the development of gas fireplaces and the ability to vent them through a wall to the outside without a masonry chimney, and the use of flexible pipe for bringing the gas to the units. Right now, it's about 50-50 wood versus gas, with wood in the living room and gas everyplace else.

In cities, gas fireplaces are used more often than wood-burning ones, especially by empty nesters moving in from the suburbs, who remember all too well what it was like dragging wood into the house to the fireplace and don't want any part of it. Where do you store the wood or get it, for that matter? If they have wood-burning fireplaces, city folk use synthetic logs.

Burning wood, of course, raises environmental issues. According to the Department of Energy (http://www.doe.gov), wood-burning appliances and fireplaces can emit large quantities of air pollutants, including nitrogen oxides, carbon monoxide, organic gases, and particulate matter. Many of these compounds can cause serious health problems, especially for children, pregnant women, and people with respiratory ailments. Several have demonstrated cancer-causing properties similar to those of cigarette smoke. In many urban and rural areas, smoke from wood burning is a major contributor to air pollution.

When a house is being completely rehabbed, getting a fireplace to work again isn't all that difficult, especially with the floors and joists exposed. If you stand in front of the fireplace, about chest-high is where it has been bricked in. You open it up, and stand back while the years of dirt and dead birds fall out. Then you drop a stainless-steel liner down from the top of the chimney, and it is ready to work again.

Most home inspectors recommend that stainless-steel liners be installed in old chimneys, because terracotta inside old chimneys tends to last only about 50 years. But liners are expensive. From top to bottom of the chimney, fourth floor to the basement, a liner costs $3,000 for about 1½ hours' work. Few companies install the liners, and when you pay, you are paying for quality.

If you have a house that was built when fireplaces were considered passé, then you have to start from scratch. Contractor John Burke owned such a house and wanted a gas fireplace. His choice: a vent-free fireplace. Burke spent a lot of time researching before he bought and installed it. The main issue was safety. A constant supply of fresh air was required to guarantee safe operation. Fortunately, the house was old and drafty. Also, the unit he bought had both a carbon monoxide monitor and an oxygen-depletion sensor. If the level of oxygen in the room with the fireplace reached a dangerous level, the flame would shut off immediately.

Wariness about vent-free appliances persists, and the units are banned in some states. Even if vent-free gas inserts and logs are permitted by the state, municipalities usually have the last word on whether they can be installed. Both nonvented and vented heating appliances must be properly maintained to reduce the risk for associated health hazards, according to the Department of Health and Human Services (http://www.dhhs.gov).

In the addition he built onto his suburban house, Burke installed a zero-clearance wood-burning fireplace in his new 40-foot-long living room. It doesn't require a masonry chimney. Instead, it has a double-wall flue, with one taking warm air from the fireplace outside and the other bringing cool air from the outside in. Tile is used inside and around the fireplace to prevent sparks from flying all over the place. The zero-clearance fireplace cost him about $1,000 and took a day to install. If you paid someone to install it for you, it would cost $1,500 to $2,000.

Electric fireplaces are making some inroads into the market, although the amount of radiant heat that plug-in fireplaces provide still remains well below the 15,000 to 40,000 BTUs that gas fireplaces generate. The typical cost of a standard gas fireplace is $600 to $3,000, without installation. Electric fireplaces run about $1,200 to $1,500, but usually generate enough heat to take the edge off one or two rooms. And they don't need venting.

48. MOVE ALONG, OLD PAINT!

As long as you have taste, redecorating can be cost-effective.

■ ■ ■

Probably the most cost-effective and least disruptive of all renovation projects is painting.

Let me backtrack here by saying it is generally cost-efficient and the least disruptive. If your house is filled with lead-based paint, it has to be removed completely, disruptively, and expensively first. Then you can go to the paint store and pick up color charts.

Paint can make a difference in so many ways, especially if some thought goes into color selection. I've inherited color sense from the previous owners of my latest house, after many years of having absolutely no sense at all.

Someone, probably a real estate agent, once told me to err on the side of neutral. So every wall that wasn't off-white in my second house was "cool gray." When I did go wild, it was on the third floor and involved a "Medici blue" teen's bedroom, a "peach" guest room, and an "alligator green" bathroom. Very few people ever saw these rooms.

In my newest house, the color sense of the previous owners manifests itself in a "potato chip" kitchen, "eucalyptus" living room and library, and "Cannon beach" bedrooms—all with white trim and off-white ceilings. In other words . . . yellow, brown, tan, and white.

Visitors leave with the names of the paint and a look at the cans.

I've learned a few rules on color over the years from talking to painters, interior decorators, and real estate agents. Dark walls (purple and dark blue) tend to make a room look smaller and absorb light, while light and neutral colors make rooms appear larger. Blue is also an appetite suppressant, however, so unless you are on a diet or are a bad cook, avoid using it in the dining room. Red is a good choice for dining rooms, because it increases the heart rate, appetite, passion, and energy.

Orange means warmth, friendliness, and welcoming, and is appropriate for living rooms and children's rooms. Violet is fine for children's rooms, because while adults find it repellent, youngsters like it. Yellow brightens a room—think of a foyer, a sunroom, or a room for the elderly—but if it is too bright, it can repel.

The trend is away from one pure color standing alone. Colors are becoming more complex and sophisticated and are incorporating a variety of special effects, including pearlescence and metallics along with the dimension of transparency and translucency. Primary, high-contrast colors appeal to children and the elderly because they define space and items best. Older, sophisticated buyers or high-end buyers prefer a complex palette, including rich chocolates or copper-orange. Ethnic buyers might respond to colors that reflect the familiar. For example, reds, oranges, and yellows are valued in Latin American countries and in Southeast Asia.

You should collect color cues from the room you want to paint. Such cues can include swatches of fabric, a piece of carpeting, or accent pieces. Take them to the color display where you buy your paint and look for families of colors that work well with those cues. By standing a few feet from the display, you can better identify the best color options.

After selecting several color cards that appeal to you, take them home so you can observe the colors where you plan to use them. Tape the paint chips to the surfaces you plan to paint, or hold the color sample at arm's length and walk around the room to see how the paint will look on different walls. Colors may look different under different lighting conditions, so be sure to assess paint colors at various times of the day and in both natural and artificial light.

If you still cannot make up your mind, you should buy small amounts of paint, apply the colors to pieces of wallboard, and view these samples where you plan to use them. Colors tend to intensify when applied to a large area. To compensate, experienced painters know that it is wise to err on the side of a lighter rather than a darker color value.

When you paint the outside of your house, you have to make a whole different set of choices. Why? Because you aren't the only person who has to live with what you do. If you live in a community with a homeowners association, the association has the last word on how the exterior of your house looks.

Homeowners also spend millions each year slapping vinyl siding on perfectly wonderful wood-sided houses, only because they hate to have to keep painting. First of all, no matter how well vinyl siding is installed, it always looks like plastic, because it is. Second, we don't know whether vinyl is relatively maintenance-free because it hasn't been around for all that long. Remember: They promised that pressure-treated lumber would last forever. They didn't tell us that what they were treating it with might be a health hazard or that we'd have to clean and recoat our treated decks with painful regularity.

For enduring exterior paint jobs, it's all in the prep work. To make the job last even longer, you'll need to keep an eye on problem areas so they don't spread, necessitating a complete repainting job. For example, if you have an area that gets more sun than the rest of the house, the paint will likely fade faster. Tackling that small area every couple of years means that you can postpone a complete and expensive paint job for more than ten years. The same applies to areas in the shade that never get a chance to dry completely and where mildew is rampant.

An exterior paint job can fall apart for several reasons. Obviously, extremes in temperature and moisture play a major role. Using incompatible primer and finish paints and buying paint of inferior quality to save money are two other reasons. Some people buy cheap paint or thin it to make it go farther, even when the manufacturer says not to. That, the experts say, will come back to haunt you.

Problems on painted surfaces manifest themselves in a variety of ways. For example, if the final coat of paint has not adhered properly to the paint beneath it, the surface of the house can look like an alligator's skin. The reasons: too many layers of paint, a badly prepped surface, or perhaps an undercoat of paint that didn't dry properly before the second coat was applied. The solution is to strip the surface to the wood, prime, and then paint. Follow the manufacturer's directions on the can.

Many exterior paints renew themselves by "chalking." The paints are manufactured so that, over time, the surface breaks down into a powdery chalk, and when it rains, the grime on the surface is washed away and the color brightens. Chalking can also occur when poor-quality paint is used or when too much time passes between paint jobs. Whatever the case, a surface that chalks will not hold a new coat of paint without preparation.

Sometimes bubbles or blisters appear on the exterior surface. If you prick the blister and find bare wood underneath, moisture has gotten under the paint. This can happen for several reasons, but the most likely is from painting in direct sunlight or over glossy surfaces. If you break the blister and there's paint underneath, the air temperature was too high when you applied the topcoat, and there was moisture behind the paint. Because of the intense heat of the sun, the trapped water vaporizes and causes a bubble. Check the manufacturer's temperature requirements on the can for the maximum recommended temperature.

How much paint will you need? To determine the amount, multiply the height in feet of your house by the perimeter and divide by 500, because one gallon of paint usually covers 500 square feet. For a new house, you typically use one primer coat and two finish coats. For an old house, it's one primer coat and one finish coat. And for every six gallons of paint for the siding, you need one gallon for the trim.

49. PARK IT THERE, PAL!

A garage offers room for expansion, for storage,
and even for the car.

■ ■ ■

My late father, Alfred R. Heavens, was a great guy with wonderful ideas, but he wasn't always successful on the follow-through.

I vividly recall the time, 40 years ago, that he decided to build me a bedroom in our garage, which was adjacent to our basement. It wasn't that he didn't park the car in the garage. He did every night. The basement, rearranged slightly, would have been a better choice for a bedroom, especially because the basement was heated directly by a furnace vent, while the garage depended on warmth provided by proximity.

No matter how many times I proposed the basement, my father would counter with the garage. Neither of us paid much attention to my mother, who argued—in retrospect, correctly—that we needed a bigger house, especially because my two sisters were sleeping in one bedroom and a third sister was due any minute.

My sisters had a large room with a bathroom. I slept in what had been the study. In that room, which was between the living room and my sisters' room, I, at 13, had absolutely no privacy. Anyone who needed to get from the living room to my sisters' room needed to go through my room. And no one in my family seemed to have heard of knocking before entering.

With an idea in his head but absolutely no plan, my father got started on the bedroom. He reasoned that I'd be a lot more comfortable if he was able to divide the garage in two with a wall between where he parked the car and where I'd be sleeping. So one Saturday morning he went to the lumberyard and bought drywall and two-by-fours.

Most people would frame the wall by nailing a header to the joists and a footer to the floor, then nailing in the studs between the two, cutting those studs to fit the space. Actually, most people would have used a tape measure, too. My father used a yardstick.

My father laid out the header and footer on the floor of the garage near the location of the wall he had marked off, and proceeded to assemble his wall, drywall and all, on the floor. Then he tried to lift his completed wall into place by himself.

My mother and I showed up to help. The wall was too tall. It became jammed at an 85-degree angle instead of the 90-degree that would have made it a wall rather than the leaning tower of Pisa. That's where it stayed, thanks to my father's unwillingness to tear out the drywall and the failure of the whole-house jack he borrowed that cracked the foundation.

Instead, we moved to a bigger house, just as my mother had said we should.

Although our garage was not ideally suited for expansion, any extra space your garage provides should not be overlooked in your renovation plans. Unfortunately, most garages have become collection areas for everything we can't fit anywhere else in the house, and before you can even begin to appropriate the space, you'll need to come up with an alternate storage site or, heaven forbid, throw a lot of the stuff away.

You've probably seen the television commercial: a couple, looking exhausted, stand in their relatively empty garage, pleased they can fit a car inside again. Then they head to their kitchen to debate the merits of canned soup. The fantasy: Folks argue over soup. The reality: There's a world full of messy garages out there.

The garage is used "as a drop-off point on the way to somewhere else in the house, because it is the closest open space," said clutter-management expert Leslie Robison of Simple Systems Organizing in Green Lane, Pennsylvania. "Then the garages end up stuffed, and people can't figure out why. Getting rid of a percentage of what's in the garage, even if it means filling a dumpster, is a crucial first step to getting it organized. It's hard to do."

Should you keep the garage as storage space for the car and all the stuff you have no room for elsewhere and try to find expansion space somewhere else in the house, or should you clean the clutter, park the car in the driveway, and build a bedroom or a home office in that space?

It depends on the alternatives. I'd never owned a garage before, but I've converted the one I now own into the workshop about which I've dreamed for 25 years. The car stays in the driveway, toward the end closest to the street. After having had to work in relatively dark, cramped basements for all those years, a garage workshop, warmed by an electric heater in the winter, was the obvious solution for my needs.

If you don't have a garage but have space for one, you should consider building one. On-site parking is at a premium in downtown areas and highly desirable in suburban ones. Covered parking is especially valued in colder climates, where it's preferable to shelter a car from the snow and cold than spend an hour getting it started and two more cleaning off the snow and ice. Also, car insurance rates tend to be lower for people who have garages in which to store their cars.

Some contractors specialize in building garages for existing houses. Cars have gotten bigger over the years, so some ten-foot-wide garages are too small. Even some new houses have smaller garages than they should. Experts suggest that a good one-car garage should be 12 by 22, while a two-car garage should be 22 by 27.

Some garages of new houses have what is known as flex space over them that allows a homeowner to expand into them. The issue, of course, is whether or not the space above the garage can be heated or air-conditioned, which itself depends on whether or not the garage has been finished. If the garage walls and floor are not insulated, then the space above the garage will be alternately too cold or too warm. To convert the flex space above the garage to living space, the issues with the garage below it, including venting for carbon monoxide to dissipate engine exhaust, need to be addressed first at additional expense.

A garage that is separate from the house that is turned into living space will need to be tied into the systems of the main house or have separate heating and cooling as well as plumbing, electricity, and telephone. If you are transforming the garage into an all-inclusive "mother-in-law" suite, renovations will be complex and expensive. My workshop garage already had electricity, and my oil-filled electric heater is usually enough to keep me warm. Only the walls and ceiling needed to be insulated and drywalled. The project cost me no more than $1,000.

Say, however, that you don't need living space as much as you need storage space, and that having storage space would free up area for expansion elsewhere in the house. As you have seen with me, garages are both project centers and storage centers, formerly a male domain centering on the automobile but now used equally by men and women, because women have begun to dominate outdoor-related tasks such as gardening. The garage is much more useful for storage than the basement because it is typically on the same level as the rest of the house.

Garage-organization products are among the fastest-growing segments of the white-hot home-organization market. Survey after survey over the last two or three years have shown that decluttering and organizing garages was high among homeowner priorities, yet garage organization is the most underserved market at the retail level. The surveys found that the same generic storage systems used in other areas of the house, other than tool systems, were being used in the garage. So more manufacturers have gotten into the garage game.

Some of the organization systems—Gladiator Garageworks by Whirlpool (http://www.whirlpool.com) is the best example—cost as much as a bathroom renovation, that is about $10,000 complete. Others cost just a few hundred dollars, which is good for most manufacturers because surveys show that the typical garage owner is willing to spend under $1,000. It depends on how much you have to store and whether, as with Gladiator, you think you need a refrigerator in your garage that matches the stainless steel of the worktops and drawers.

One way to organize the garage, as opposed to the rest of the house, is to view the area as a series of systems. Most projects are tackled in steps. If the garage is designed the same way, the homeowner moves from one station to the next, while maximizing time and productivity. A mechanic might use an 18-foot wall most effectively to store a chest and a rollaway unit loaded with hand and portable power tools; a compressor with easy access to air tools for installing, sanding, spraying, or disassembling parts; a workbench for tabletop activity and construction projects; and a vertical cabinet to store cleaners, extension cords, trouble lights, and other essentials.

Bottom line: Whether you use it as living space, work space, or storage area, make sure that you make the best use of your garage. A well-planned garage will easily turn wasted space into efficient, useful space. And, who knows? You may even be able to fit in the car.

50. HOW DOES YOUR GARDEN GROW?

Landscaping is a relatively inexpensive way to add value
to your house.

■ ■ ■

I was waiting to tape my Gadgeteer segment on the Discovery Channel's *Home Matters* program a couple of years back, when the landscape expert scheduled to appear on the same show marched up to me.

"You the real estate guy?" he demanded, pointing his finger in my face.

"That's me," I replied, bracing for the punch yet wondering whether I should start calling myself "The Real Estate Guy" professionally.

"Tell your readers that landscaping is the key ingredient in selling a house," he shouted, startling the dessert expert and the pet doctor who were waiting with me.

The landscape expert marched out of the room.

"What's up with him?" the dessert expert asked me.

"Some professionals take their jobs seriously," I said, thumbing through a copy of her latest book and licking the pages.

The landscape expert was correct, although a bit overzealous. According to the National Association of Realtors (http://www.realtors .org), about 50 percent of all house sales are based on first impressions from the curb. While a lot of that has to do with the physical condition of the houses in question—roses can't always hide a rotting porch, no matter how hard I've tried—properly maintained landscaping contributes greatly to the marketability.

In addition, landscaping projects, if properly planned and kept under control, can be cost-effective. Landscaping will enhance the look of your house for potential buyers as well as bring you virtually limitless pleasure, if you maintain it. As with everything else home-related, you cannot just plant and walk away from your creation. It has to be watered and weeded regularly. Even if you do the right thing, your garden may still die, and you'll need to start over.

The trouble is, landscaping changes cannot be made overnight. Plants, like humans, need to put down roots and grow. Although I have tried to emphasize throughout this book that you should not renovate just to sell, a lot of people do it anyway. What they discover is that you can't decide to put a house on the market next month and think that you can re-create the Garden of Eden by the time prospective buyers drive by. Miracle-Gro® just doesn't work that fast. And, as Cher's character Loretta Camarari said in the movie *Moonstruck,* "This is modern times. There ain't no more miracles."

Considering everything that can go wrong—squirrels eat the hundreds of bulbs you've planted throughout the winter, bugs destroy the rest in the spring, the apple trees attract yellow jackets, and prolonged drought and water conservation measures turn your lawn into a desert—why do we even bother? The reason is that humans feel a constant impulse to transform nature into something we can understand. We garden because we can't understand nature. And, although we think we create the garden, the garden actually re-creates us.

That's the philosophical reason, anyway. Most of us just hope what we do will look pretty.

If you are planning major renovation work, especially a large addition, you'll need to wait until the project has been completed before you begin landscaping. That doesn't mean that you should not start thinking about what you will want to plant and where. It means that you shouldn't be competing for space with the backhoe operator digging the foundation. Even if you plant that curly willow tree you've craved far from the addition, it will be just your luck that the contractor will want to run a new water line or gas connection right through the tree.

If it were me, I'd wait until the addition has been completed and the workers are gone. I would then need to decide whether I should simply extend the existing landscaping to the addition or I should tear everything out and start over. No matter what I do, I need to ensure that the landscaping ties in the addition to the original house, a critical point, I believe, for a couple of reasons. First, you should de-emphasize the difference between new and old. Your goal is to tie the original to the addition seamlessly, so that anyone who looks at your house cannot tell the difference. Second, if you were unable to use the same materials to cover both—perhaps the original has cedar siding, but the addition is sided with vinyl that mimics the more costly cedar—proper landscaping can de-emphasize the differences in the material by capturing the observer's attention.

If you are satisfied with what you already have, I strongly suggest that you do everything you can to preserve it. Only recently, when confronted with a growing tide of anti-sprawl sentiment that can affect their bottom lines, have residential builders tried to preserve as much plant life as possible. Many of them actually have trees dug up and stored until they can be replanted, which is something that you can negotiate with your contractor on a smaller scale. You also can adjust your plans to ensure that trees and shrubs are preserved, and you can include a provision in your contract stating that anything the work damages or destroys will be replaced—within reason, of course.

It's taken me 22 years and three houses to design a front yard I can live with, but if you are lucky enough to hit on a perfect plan, it might take you only a year or two. If you have cash to spare, I suggest you hire a landscape architect, give them a laundry list, sketch something out on the back of an envelope, and see what you get. For most of us, however, gardening is hit or miss. The experimentation is the most fun.

While most of what goes into my garden comes from nearby nurseries, I'm always on the lookout for the unusual. One time, I came across a garden center that grows exotic perennial wildflowers in its greenhouses. I bought several varieties, and they truly enhanced the landscape. I also spend part of the early fall looking for bargains as the nurseries begin selling off their stock. Fall is an ideal time to plant. It also is the best time to reseed the lawn. I also have gotten on the mailing lists of dozens of seed catalog companies, and I often contact local arboretums and university extension services for free advice.

And here's another piece of advice: make sure you take photographs of your yard when it looks its best. That way, if you have to sell your house in the dead of winter, you have proof that it looks wonderful the rest of the year.

As I've tried to emphasize, even people with green thumbs can't be successful gardeners all the time. Nature can be cruel, yet that cruelty often stems from the fact that we've tried to break nature's rules. One of those is introducing plants from other regions into our landscape. For example, if you import a plant from the tropics to the desert Southwest, that plant will likely require much more water than the plants native to the region. Because water is so precious, there is no return on your investment in the tropical plant, no matter how exotic it is.

The solution, of course, is to grow things native to the area. You don't waste water and face the threat of not having enough for the plant and your own needs. You also perpetuate native species, and you also don't introduce pests and diseases for which the local plants have no defense. Having native plants also encourages the continuation of native birds that dine on the local bugs, which also find the plants attractive.

There are other reasons for landscaping. Exchanging grass and trees for pavement can result in global warming, or at least raise the temperature locally. That's why cities are hotter than the suburbs in the summer. If you fill in ponds and streams to build, reducing water's cooling effect also raises the temperature. If you want to consider the problem even more locally, altering the landscape can reduce the drainage on your property, which means that the nice addition on which you've spent $100,000 might start taking on water in heavy rainstorms.

Fixing that problem would be much more expensive than planting a few shrubs.

■ THINGS TO REMEMBER

76. Incorporating universal design into your renovation will keep you in your house and independent as you age.

77. Universal design changes will not affect the resale value of your house. In fact, as the population ages, they may add to the value.

78. Unless you operate a business at home, don't spend bushels of money on a home office. The expense isn't justified, and the return is the same, no matter what you do.

79. Double-flushing defeats the purpose of a low-flow toilet.

80. If you can possibly save your existing 3.5-gallon toilet in a renovation, do it. You can find other, better ways of reducing water use.

81. Increasing the diameter of the flush valve on a low-flow toilet seems to prevent clogging.

82. When replacing toilet parts, check out whether using generic parts will compromise the operation of the fixture.

83. A deck lasts an average of 11 years.

84. About once a decade, a homeowner expands, upgrades, or replaces a deck.

85. Lumber treated with chromated copper arsenate (CCA) is no longer permitted for residential use.

86. Decks made of CCA-treated lumber don't need to be replaced. They should be cleaned and sealed regularly and safely.

87. Most decks are smaller than they should be. Add a couple of feet to your design. You'll use every inch.

88. The deck should be an extension of the living space, not an appendage to the house.

89. Always get the proper permits for deck construction.

90. Tankless water heaters, properly sized and installed, can provide an uninterrupted flow of hot water on demand.

91. Tankless heaters, less susceptible to corrosion, can last five to ten years longer than storage-type models.

92. Reliable home security is a blend of technology and common sense.

93. A burglar alarm system that is continually monitored by a security company will reduce the cost of your homeowners insurance.

94. A basement laundry room can actually reduce the sale price of your house.

95. Second-floor laundry rooms attract older buyers and families with teenage children.

96. No basement is ever completely dry.

97. Depending on where you live, swimming pools often cost more to build and maintain than they add in value.

98. Energy efficiency is not the only consideration in replacing windows. Whatever you install should not detract from the overall appearance of the house.

99. Everyone wants a fireplace. However, gas fireplaces are more efficient and involve less maintenance than wood-burning models.

100. Painting is the most cost-effective and least disruptive renovation project.

I have come to depend on the Internet for the most up-to-date information available and the widest number and variety of sources. You should, too. Typing a keyword such as *kitchen* into a search engine and then continually refining that search—for example, *kitchen cabinet hardware European style*—will usually bring you what you need.

Although I have read many home improvement books over the years, I own few. The ones I do have on the shelf I turn to when I'm looking for ideas or am truly stumped on a problem. There are two general-information books that I recommend you buy:

1. *Home Book: The Ultimate Guide to Repairs, Improvements, and Maintenance.* Creative Homeowner, $40. (http://www .creativehomeowner.com).
2. Black & Decker's *The Complete Guide to Home Improvement.* Creative Publishing International, $34.95.

There are a lot of shelter magazines on the market. Most of them are, frankly, form over substance. They may be pretty, but they aren't very useful or practical and can often mislead you about the complexity and cost of projects. I write or have written for some of them. Important content is usually sacrificed for pretty pictures. And believe me, in renovation, one illustration is not worth five words, let alone a thousand, when the picture it presents is misleading.

The shelter magazines that are spin-offs of television shows are designed primarily to promote those shows and typically provide a record of the same information you could get by turning on your VCR.

Two magazines I trust and keep as reference are:

1. *Old-House Journal.* Publishes six issues a year at $3.95 each. The style can be a little preachy sometimes, but the expertise in its pages is well worth the price.
2. *Fine Homebuilding.* Published monthly by Taunton Press at $6.95 per issue. Primarily written by contractors or former craftspeople, it provides firsthand knowledge in a readable, easily understandable manner.

Both magazines are excellent sources of hard-to-find materials, such as tile that matches the kind in the bathroom floor you've just had to rip out.

Although *Remodeling* magazine, published by Hanley-Wood, is written primarily for those involved in the industry, its annual "Cost versus Value" report offers some insight into what home improvement projects might cost and what kind of return a homeowner can expect to get on the investment when the house is sold sometime down the road. The report is available at http://www.remodeling .hw.net and other Web sites. A word of warning: The report is a guide only. The costs and returns are based on what real estate agents and contractors in various areas of the country have reported. Your project costs and returns could differ by thousands of dollars.

Thanks to the advent of cable, there are more shelter-related television shows than you can shake your fist at. I know that after watching most of them, I want to shake my fist.

The best, for my money and limited time, is *Hometime*. No other show has come as close to providing as much practical information to me over the years. The rest of what you need is on the Internet.

GOVERNMENT RESOURCES

- *U.S. Department of Energy* (http://www.doe.gov) is the key to energy-saving construction techniques and products, including Energy Star products such as washers, dryers, and air conditioners.
- *The U.S. Department of Housing and Urban Development* (http://www.hud.gov) has lots of information on how to buy a house, how to finance renovations, how to avoid contractor scams, and how to deal with hazardous materials such as lead-based paint.
- *The U.S. Department of Environmental Protection* (http://www .epa.gov) has the latest data on health hazards and indoor air quality.
- *The U.S. Consumer Products Safety Commission* (http://www .cpsc.gov) is also a mine of information on what works, what breaks easily, and how dangerous products can be.

For information on local and state regulations that deal with permits, building codes, disposal of hazardous waste, and licensing requirements for companies doing business in your area, you should make use of your search engine.

Fannie Mae (http://www.fanniemae.com) and Freddie Mac (http:// www.freddiemac.com) are quasi-governmental providers of funds to lenders for mortgage products, including renovation loans. Their Web sites are also mines of information on how to determine the kind of loan that fits your needs as well as the pitfalls of renovation loans. You can find the lenders with which these two agencies deal via direct links from their Web sites, in most cases.

ASSOCIATIONS

Although they exist to present the points of view of their groups, Web sites of many real estate and home improvement associations are sources of information that, when used properly, can be invaluable to you.

- American Homeowners Association (http://www.aha.org)
- The American Bar Association (http://www.abanet.org)
- The National Association of Realtors (http://www.realtor.org)
- The National Association of Home Builders (http://www.nahb.com)
- The National Association of the Remodeling Industry (http://www.nari.org)
- The American Association of Home Inspectors (http://www.ashi.org)
- The National Association of Home Inspectors (http://www.nahi.org)
- The Plumbing, Heating, and Cooling Contractors Association (http://www.phccweb.org)
- The American Institute of Architects (http://www.aia.org)
- The National Kitchen and Bath Association (http://www.nkba.org)
- Underwriters Laboratories (http://www.ul.com)
- The National Fire Protection Association (http://www.nfpa.org)
- Institute of Electrical and Electronics Engineers (http://www.ieee.org)
- National Electrical Contractors Association (http://www.neca.org)
- American Society of Heating, Refrigeration, and Air Conditioning Engineers (http://www.ahrae.org)
- The Insurance Information Institute (http://www.iii.org)
- The Window and Door Manufacturers Association (http://www.wdma.org)
- National Association of Energy Service Companies (http://www.naesc.org)
- American Water Works Association (http://www.awwa.org)
- American Gas Association (http://www.aga.org)
- National Pool and Spa Association (http://www.npsa.org)

- Alliance to Save Energy (http://www.ase.org)
- Association of Home Appliance Manufacturers (http://www.aham.org)
- The Brick Institute of America (http://www.bia.org)
- The National Hardwood Lumber Association (http://www.nhla.org)
- The Southern Pine Council (http://www.southernpine.com)
- Efficient Windows Collaborative (http://www.efficientwindows.org)
- Hearth, Patio and Barbecue Association (http://www.hpba.org)
- Chimney Safety Institute (http://www.csia.org)

MORE USEFUL WEB SITES

- The Rohm & Haas Paint Quality Institute (http://www.paintquality.com)
- The Portland Cement Association (http://www.pce.org)
- The NAHB Research Center (http://www.nahbrc.org)
- The Appraisal Institute (http://www.api.org)
- National Safety Council (http://www.nsc.org)

These Web sites come with no guarantees. Just look at them to see if they are helpful.

- http://www.contractor.com—Provides an idea of what various projects can cost.
- http://www.improvenet.com—Matches you with contractors specializing in your job in your area.
- http://www.repairclinic.com—Describes how to fix and where to find parts.
- http://www.cornerhardware.com—This is another place to find parts.

Appliance and fixture manufacturers also have Web sites from which you can choose, from the convenience of your desk, the right product to meet your needs. Some even let you order and buy the product. Always shop around for lower prices and the best service before you buy.

Use that search engine.

INDEX

A

Abram, Norm, 4, 32
Accessibility, 155–59
Additions, 8, 43
Air cleaners, 126, 129
Air-conditioning, 82, 144, 151, 181
Air quality, 126–30
Air-to-air heat exchangers, 129
Alarm systems (burglar), 176–78, 208
Allergies, 126–30
Alliance to Save Energy, 163, 189, 190
Aluminum windows, 188
American Express Company, 11
American Lung Association, 129
American Society of Appraisers, 105
American Water Works Association
　Research Foundation, 164
Appliances, 5
Appliance Statistical Review, 101
Appraisers
　for home contents, 105–6
　insurance, 103–4
Appraisers Association of America, 105
Arbitration, 92
Architects, 57–59, 107
Architectural integrity, 95–96, 109, 189
Argon gas, 190
Arsenic, 169–70
Asbestos, 115–16, 120
Assertiveness, 74–75
Attics, 8, 135–36, 137, 150

B

Barbone, Noelle, 187
Barrier-free renovations, 155–59
Basement(s), 9
　insulation and, 137
　laundry rooms in, 179, 208
　mold and, 124
　storage and, 183
　water and, 23, 181–84, 208
Bathroom(s)
　accessibility and, 156–57
　caulking, 25
　plumbing and, 139
　tankless water heaters and, 173
　toilets, 163–67
　water conservation and, 141
　wiring and, 133
Bennett, Laura Philips, 71–73
Better Homes and Gardens, 40
Bio-Charge, 140
Bonding, 91
Bonus rooms, 9
Building codes, 59, 67
　laundry rooms and, 180–81
　local nature of, 82
　violations of, 81
Burglar alarm system, 176–78, 208
Burglary Prevention Council, 178
Burke, John, 193
BX wiring, 133